sharing deep insights earned from life on the existential knife's edge."

—Naomi Klein, author of *How to Change Everything: The Young Human's Guide to Protecting the Planet and Each Other*

"Powerful with love, and tender about what it needs to be tender about, and direct, even fierce where it means to tell us what we need to be thinking about what we've been doing to this world, to Aguon's people, and to Indigenous people everywhere, to the land and to all its beings . . . as the dying eight-spot butterfly he writes about, strong and luminous as a needed beacon in a fog of disinformation and dismay, Julian Aguon with this small book emerges already a giant."

—Tommy Orange, author of *There There*

"A breathtaking book and I mean it—this book took my breath away . . . alive with passion, wisdom, and heart, you can almost feel its pulse. A call not only for justice but for a brand-new covenant with our world."

—Junot Díaz, author of *The Brief Wondrous Life of Oscar Wao*

"Inspired spiritual and practical wisdom from a Guam lawyer/poet/seer that transmits ways of knowing, feeling, and acting, which speak directly to the mind and heart of everyone on the planet. If reading this short book doesn't change your life, nothing will."

—Richard Falk, author of *Public Intellectual: The Life of a Citizen Pilgrim*

"Aguon's pen is a spear. He has the unerring ability to pierce the heart of any matter he writes about, from colonialism to climate change, and he writes in a way that both exposes horrors and expresses love to the young."

—Noenoe K. Silva, author of *Aloha Betrayed*

"This book is a gift—full of beauty, truth telling, and love. This book will enlighten and inspire anyone interested in understanding and doing something about colonialism, capitalism, racism, militarism, war, and violence of all kinds. As importantly, this book will move you emotionally. It will move you to change how you live your life. It will move you to help change the world for the better."

—David Vine, author of *The United States of War*

"Aguon is one of Oceania's most important thinkers who uses his ability to see through complicated systems to fight for our islands and peoples. With razor-sharp analysis and a ton of heart, he both defends and calls forth our communities. I will regularly return to this book for inspiration—to remind me why I do my own work."

—Kathy Jetñil-Kijiner, author of *Iep Jaltok: Poems from a Marshallese Daughter*

"Aguon's work transcends all boundaries and centers Indigenous relationships to people and place. Whether drawing on his legal or poetic skills, Aguon reckons with the rage and violence of colonialism while gently unfolding a new vision for justice and healing."

—Holly Barker, author of *Bravo for the Marshallese*

"Aguon gifts us, in shrunken times, the Indigenous version of the all-encompassing vision that Aristotle and his disciple Aquinas bequeathed humanity: truth equals beauty equals goodness."

—Maivân Lâm, author of *At the Edge of the State*

"What an incredible gift. This book is a powerful spiritual remix, a multi-scalar tapestry of love, kinship, resistance, and creative survival from Oceania. His tribute to our late elder sister, Teresia, brought tears of grief and joy. Ko bati n rabwa Julian, 'we will live . . . on our own terms.'"

—Katerina Martina Teaiwa, author of *Consuming Ocean Island*

"A celebration of Indigenous hope and survival amid the destructive and desecrating forces of militarism, capitalism, and climate change, and a provocation for collective action for just and sustainable futures in the Marianas—a must read for anyone interested in the beauty of Indigenous worlds and struggles for liberation!"

—Christine Taitano DeLisle, author of *Placental Politics*

"Reading this collection reminds me of being immersed in our ocean. The sunlight that illuminates the water cannot be held, and yet to behold the ways rays and sea dance together opens the soul . . . Aguon is one of Oceania's most brilliant advocates and expansive voices—a voice that urgently needs to be heard."

   —Noelani Goodyear-Kaʻōpua, author of
   The Seeds We Planted

"Aguon tells the Chamorro story by merging a profound love for our Indigenous people and culture with his potent intellect and creative genius."

   —Anne Perez Hattori, author of *Colonial Dis-Ease*

"A devastatingly gentle song of resistance."

   —Jonathan K. K. Osorio, author of *Dismembering Lāhui*

No Country for Eight-Spot Butterflies

NO COUNTRY FOR EIGHT-SPOT BUTTERFLIES

A LYRIC ESSAY

Julian Aguon

ASTRA HOUSE ⋀ New York

Photographs provided courtesy of the author.

Astra House
A Division of Astra Publishing House
astrahouse.com
Printed in the United States of America

Library of Congress Cataloging-in-Publication Data

Names: Aguon, Julian, author.

Title: No country for eight-spot butterflies : a lyric essay / Julian Aguon.

Description: First edition. | New York : Astra House, [2022] | Includes bibliographical references. | Summary: "No Country for Eight-Spot Butterflies is a collection of soulful ruminations about love, loss, struggle, resilience and power. Part memoir, part manifesto, the book is both a coming-of-age story and a call for justice-for everyone but, in particular, for indigenous peoples-his own and others"—Provided by publisher.

Identifiers: LCCN 2022002991 (print) | LCCN 2022002992 (ebook) | ISBN 9781662601637 (hardcover) | ISBN 9781662601644 (epub)

Subjects: LCSH: Aguon, Julian. | Chamorro (Micronesian people)—Guam—Biography. | Civil rights lawyers—Guam—Biography. | Chamorro (Micronesian people)—Guam—Social conditions. | Indigenous peoples—Social conditions. | Social justice. | Environmental justice.

Classification: LCC DU647 .A593 2022 (print) | LCC DU647 (ebook) | DDC 305.89/9952—dc23/eng/20220225

LC record available at https://lccn.loc.gov/2022002991

LC ebook record available at https://lccn.loc.gov/2022002992

First edition

10 9 8 7 6 5 4 3 2 1

Design by Richard Oriolo

The text is set in Adobe Caslon Pro.

The titles are set in Trade Gothic LT Std Bold.

For Ron—who taught me what
it means to have blood in my eyes

"I want to sing like the birds sing, not worrying about who hears or what they think."

—RUMI

CONTENTS

Introduction by Arundhati Roy   1

The Properties of Perpetual Light   3

Go with the Moon   7

No Country for Eight-Spot Butterflies   8

My Mother's Bamboo Bracelets: A Handful of Lessons on
Saving the World   14

Sherman Alexie Looked Me Dead in the Eye Once   21

More Right   24

Birthday Cakes Mean Birthdays   26

Yugu Means Yoke   31

A Crowbar and a Conch Shell   35

The Gift Anne Gave Me   38

Nirmal Hriday   42

Mugo'   46

The Ocean Within   48

We Have No Need for Scientists   54

We Reach for You   57

Reflections While Driving   58

Nikki and Me   63

Onion and Garlic   66

Fighting Words   69

Yeye Tere   78

Our Father   81

Gaosåli   88

Curved Sticks and Cowrie Shells: A Conversation
between Julian Aguon & Desiree Taimanglo-Ventura   90

AFTERWORD   101
REFERENCES   105
ACKNOWLEDGMENTS   107
ABOUT THE AUTHOR   109

No Country for Eight-Spot Butterflies

Introduction
By Arundhati Roy

OFTEN, IN moments of despair, I think of us, the human race, all packed into a public bus that is hurtling toward the edge of a cliff while we bicker over which songs to sing.

Perhaps we can at least agree to stop that squabbling now—because here's a song book for us, with songs that are worth singing out loud. Even if we're going down.

No Country for Eight-Spot Butterflies (or, for that matter swiftlets, starlings, or slender-toed geckoes) is testimony to the music of survival in a tone-deaf world, of poetry amid a language heist, of tenderness in the face of myriad forms of relentless violence with the annihilation-of-everything coded into it. Julian Aguon offers the kind of intelligence that has been eroded, almost to extinction, by another, far baser form of intelligence, narrowed, blunted, weaponized, and harnessed wholly in the service of modern capitalism and its ideas of progress and happiness.

There are songs of love here, deeply personal as well as epic and political.

There are songs of rage and resistance.

Songs of death and redemption.

Songs of extinction.

Songs of oceans and islands, drowning songs, swimming songs, fish songs, fuck-you songs.

And then there are the footnotes that make you laugh and cry. Love letters, ridiculous anecdotes, and a description of how the author peed with joy after reading the climax of a book he loved.

This book is an embrace.

—ARUNDHATI ROY

PS: I wrote this very short introduction because I wanted to formally and officially be included in its embrace. Even if we're going down.

The Properties of Perpetual Light

THE WRITERS I love most are almost always on a mission. To save the world one sentence at a time. To redeem us and to rescue back our righteous minds. These writers risk not only the criticism of their peers (as earnestness is said to ruin art) but also the possibility that their words will be mangled and misunderstood. Still they offer up their gifts, hoping, as the brilliant black feminist Audre Lorde had hoped, that their words can close some of the gap between blindness[1] and our better selves. In other words, these writers do language, but they also do battle.

And the battle is on.

Whether we like it or not—whether we choose to deny it or not—climate change has put us on an unforgiving timeline. If the Intergovernmental Panel on Climate Change (IPCC) Special Report on Global Warming of 1.5°C is to be believed, we have about eight years left to get our collective shit together, curb our emissions, and ensure the future habitability of the earth. Ensure there is a future.

---

[1]Of course, I don't mean to invoke blindness in an ableist sense, such that having a visual disability is equated with not being able to understand, recognize what matters, or think deeply. Rather, I appreciate Audre Lorde's insight about oppressed people—that we are "always being asked to stretch a little more, to bridge the gap between blindness and humanity." Ms. Lorde was a boss who leaned into her power, made profound intellectual contributions to the cause of racial and gender justice, and suffered absolutely no fools.

And the questions fall to the soul like dew to the pasture.[2]

Where do we go from here? What do we do with our desolation? How obscene is it that communities with the smallest carbon footprint—like low-lying islands and atolls in the middle of the Pacific Ocean—are paying the steepest price for a crisis we had almost no hand in creating? How do warm-blooded longings for equity and justice figure into global discourse dominated by the cold language of mitigation and adaptation? How do we stay sane as well as sentient? As the luminous author-activist Naomi Klein puts it, how do we stay human in a warming world?

This book, sadly, does not answer any of these questions. Not directly anyway.

This collection instead attempts to trace the arc of the morally strenuous spirit that drives so many writers to take pen to paper. It is an homage of sorts to the work of the activist-writer, which is the work of bearing witness, wrestling with the questions of one's day, telling children the truth.

This book collates a wide range of writing, penned for various audiences, to mark a variety of occasions—from graduations and protests to birthdays and funerals. Even an impending nuclear threat. Some of these pieces were not originally intended to be shared but rather were adapted from old notes and journal entries, written at particularly memorable moments in my life. What connects all of them

---

[2]A line borrowed from Pablo Neruda's poem, "Tonight I Can Write," from his gorgeous collection, *Twenty Love Poems and a Song of Despair.* I will always be indebted to my Kashmiri friend, Erfana, who not only introduced me to Neruda, but who took me along whenever she'd go swimming in his sentences.

is not their subject matter but their spirit, which more than anything else is a spirit of insistence. All of them, in their own way, insist on life, no matter the hour, even at the hour of death.

There is a Catholic prayer for the dead that children in Guam learn early on, our parents having dragged us to more rosaries than we can remember. While the prayer is beloved by Catholics everywhere, here we cradle it closer than most, if only because there is just so much death. When a loved one dies, we descend upon a family member's home (or the village church) to pray for nine nights. In unison, we say:

Eternal rest grant unto them, O Lord.
And let perpetual light shine upon them.
May they rest in peace.

I have recited these words thousands of times, yet it is only now, in compiling this manuscript, that I have truly reflected on their meaning.

In one of the entries included here (a commencement speech I gave to the graduating class of my former high school), I talk about how reading Paulo Coelho's *The Alchemist* recalibrated my thinking about what it means to be a self-actualized adult—and what it takes to become one. In the speech, I tell the graduates that the only way to successfully make the journey (from adolescence to adulthood) is to learn how to "get quiet"—that is, to quiet down the noise of other people's opinions and to take instruction instead from one's own heart.

I tell them of a beautiful exchange between the alchemist and the boy after days of traveling the desert, where the alchemist explains that those who are interested only in gold do not understand the secret of alchemy—for lead, copper, and iron all have their own destinies to fulfill, and anyone who interferes with another's destiny will never discover her own.

This exchange has stayed with me. Like a pressing on the chest.

I think I finally know why.

In our spiritual lives as much as our material ones, the same insight applies. In the same way that the earth metals have different properties, so too do their spiritual counterparts like hope and faith. What is hope, for instance, if not a stubborn chink of light in the dark? What is faith if not setting out in that same darkness with only our belief in the light to guide us?

And what of *perpetual* light? What are its properties?

We know from the Bible that the only thing to ever precede light is love.

I think that's it.

Perpetual Light is the Ancient Beauty.

When we recite the prayer for the dead, we are asking God for our loved one's safe passage, and we are offering up the only thing we have, our love, to light their way.

This book is a little like that. Like a love letter to young people.

It seeks to call them forth. To do language and to do battle.

To write as if everything they love is on the line.

Because it is.

Go with the Moon

GO WITH the moon, my godfather says.

He's a talayeru, meaning he throws net and he knows things.

Like what time of year the mañahak run, which is the actual question I asked.

"Seriously, Ninu?" I say.

"Seriously," he says. "You get your gear ready in April 'cause that's the first run. Late April into early May. You get seven days, maybe ten, but that's it, so you gotta be ready."

Then he self-corrects. Tells me those months don't matter, not really anyway. Tells me, for the second time, that what matters is the moon.

"The last quarter moon, the real thin one, that's the one we want," he says, his voice trailing, his eyes fixed on a grayish blob moving in the distance.

I don't ask any more questions.

Just watch.

Watch the gray blob, which is really a school of baby rabbitfish, come into focus. Watch a quiet man grow quieter. Watch a white net spread itself out like a circular dream. And drop.

And I am in awe.

Never ever have I seen something so quiet be so alive.

No Country for Eight-Spot Butterflies

IN GUAM, even the dead are dying.

As I write this, the US Department of Defense is ramping up the militarization of my homeland—part of its $8 billion scheme to relocate roughly 5,000 Marines from Okinawa to Guam. In fact, ground has already been broken along the island's beautiful northern coastline for a massive firing range complex. The complex—consisting of five live-fire training ranges and support facilities—is being built dangerously close to the island's primary source of drinking water, the Northern Guam Lens Aquifer. Moreover, the complex is situated over several historically and culturally significant sites, including the remnants of ancient villages several thousands of years old, where our ancestors' remains remain.

The construction of these firing ranges will entail the destruction of more than 1,000 acres of native limestone forest. These forests are unbearably beautiful, took millennia to evolve, and today function as essential habitat for several endangered endemic species, including a fruit bat, a flightless rail, and three species of tree snails—not to mention a swiftlet, a starling, and a slender-toed gecko. The largest of the five ranges, a 59-acre multipurpose machine-gun range,

will be built a mere 100 feet from the last remaining repro-
ductive håyon lågu tree in Guam.

If only superpowers were concerned with the stuff of low-
ercase earth—like forests and fresh water. If only they were
curious about *the whisper and scurry of small lives*.[3] If only they
were moved by beauty.

If only.

But the militarization of Guam is nothing if not proof that
they are not so moved. In fact, the military buildup now
underway is happening over the objections of thousands of the
island's residents. Many of these protestors, including myself,
are Indigenous Chamorros whose ancestors endured five
centuries of colonization and who see this most recent wave
of unilateral action by the United States simply as the latest
course in a long and steady diet of dispossession.

When the US Navy first released its highly technical (*and
11,000-page-long*) Draft Environmental Impact Statement in
November 2009, the people of Guam submitted over 10,000
comments outlining our concerns, many of us strenuously
opposed to the military's plans. We produced simplified edu-
cational materials on the anticipated adverse impacts of
those plans, and provided community trainings on them. We
took hundreds of people hiking through the jungles specifically slated for destruction. We took several others swimming
in the harbor where the military proposed dredging some
40 acres of coral reef for the berthing of a nuclear-powered

---

[3]A phrase borrowed from Arundhati Roy's sublime debut novel, *The God of Small Things*.

aircraft carrier. We testified so many times and in so many ways, in the streets and in the offices of elected officials. We even filed a lawsuit under the National Environmental Policy Act, effectively forcing the navy to conduct further environmental impact assessments, thus pushing the buildup back a few years.

But delay was all we won and the bulldozers are back with a vengeance.

A $78 million contract for the live-fire training range complex has been awarded to Black Construction, which has already begun clearing 89 acres of primary limestone forest and 110 acres of secondary limestone forest. It's bitterly ironic that so many of these machines bear the name "Caterpillar" when the very thing they are destroying is that precious creature's preciously singular habitat. To be sure, such forests house the host plants for the endemic Mariana eight-spot butterfly. But then again maybe a country that routinely prefers power over strength, and living over letting live, is no country for eight-spot butterflies.

While this wave of militarization should elicit our every outrage, indignation is not nearly enough to build a bridge. To anywhere. It's useful, yes. But we need to get a hell of a lot more serious about articulating alternatives if we hope to withstand the forces of predatory global capitalism and ultimately replace its ethos of extraction with one of our own. In the case of my own people, an ethos of reciprocity.

And nowhere is that ethos more alive than in those very same forests—for it is there that our yo'åmte, or healers, are perpetuating our culture, in particular our traditional healing practices. It is there on the forest floor and in the crevices of the limestone rock that many of the plants needed to make our medicine grow. It is there that our medicine women gather the plants their mothers, and their mothers' mothers, gathered before them.

These plants, combined with others harvested from elsewhere on the island, treat everything from anxiety to arthritis. As someone who suffers from regular bouts of bronchitis, I can attest to the fact that the medicine Auntie Frances Arriola Cabrera Meno makes to treat respiratory problems has proven more effective in my case than any medicine of the modern world. Yet Auntie Frances, like so many other yo'åmte I know, takes no credit for the cure. As she tells it, to do so would be hubris, as so many others are involved in the healing process: the plants themselves, with whom she converses in a secret language; her mother, who taught her how to identify which plants have which properties and also how and when to pick them; and the ancestors, who give her permission to enter the jungle and who, on occasion, favor her, allowing her to find everything she needs and more.

More than this, she tells me that I too am part of that process—that people like me, who seek out her services, give her life meaning. That she wouldn't know what to do with herself if she wasn't making medicine. That the life of a healer was always hers to have because she was born breech under a new moon and thus had the hands for healing.

But such things are inevitably lost in translation. And no military on earth is sensitive enough to perceive something as soft as the whisper of another worldview.

Earlier this month, I received an invitation to serve on the Global Advisory Council for Progressive International—a new and exciting global initiative to mobilize people around the world behind a shared vision of social justice.[4]

So of course I said yes.

Truth be told, I know little by way of details—what kind of time commitment are we talking about? how will we work as a group? who else said yes?—but I am ready anyway.[5] Ready to build a global justice movement that is anchored, at least in part, in the intellectual contributions of Indigenous peoples. Peoples who have a unique capacity to resist despair through connection to collective memory and who just might be our best hope to build a new world rooted in reciprocity and mutual respect—for the earth and for each other. The world we need. The world of our dreams.

---

[4] Our mission is to build a planetary front of progressive forces, with progressive defined as the aspiration to a world that is: democratic, decolonized, just, egalitarian, liberated, solidaristic, sustainable, ecological, peaceful, post-capitalist, prosperous, and plural. Since May 2020, we've grown to include unions, parties, and movements representing millions of people around the world, from the National Alliance of People's Movements in India to the Congreso de los Pueblos in Colombia to the Democracy in Europe Movement, or DiEM 25. We've launched international campaigns on issues like debt cancellation in the Global South, developed a policy vision for "Reclaiming the World After Covid-19," and built a wire service for the translation and dissemination of critical perspectives shut out by mainstream media around the world.

[5] I've since learned the identity of the other 50+ Global Advisory Council members. They include such luminaries as Naomi Klein, Noam Chomsky, Cornel West, Nikhil Dey, Aruna Roy, Nick Estes, Ece Temelkuran, Céline Semaan, Tasneem Essop, Ahdaf Soueif, Hilda Heine, and others. To say it's an honor to be among them is an understatement.

The same world who, on a quiet day in September, bent down low and breathed in the ear of Arundhati Roy.

She is still on her way.[6]

---

[6] A reference to the famous closing passage of Arundhati Roy's "Come September" speech. As you will probably gather by the time you're done reading this book, I love Arundhati Roy to an almost ridiculous degree. Love the masterpiece that is *The God of Small Things*. Love her nonfiction even more. Love her naturally adversarial relationship with power. Love that she once referred to herself as a "cappist" and a "liddite." Love her insistence that the very smallest of things connect to the very biggest. Love that she once burst into tears in a market in Delhi upon seeing a whole plate of different kinds of lentils—because globalization means standardization and she's a defender of difference, wilderness, and wild beauty. Toward the top of my bucket list of stupidly wonderful things to do before I die—*e.g., listening to Joni Mitchell's* Blue *album beneath the Northern Lights in Iceland in winter; playing soccer at sunset with Bob Marley's descendants on a wide-open field in Jamaica*— is rendezvousing with Arundhati on a houseboat on Dal Lake in Srinagar, Kashmir, or on a high terrace anywhere in India, eating mangoes in the moonlight.

My Mother's Bamboo Bracelets:
A Handful of Lessons on Saving the World

The following is a commencement address I gave in May 2009 to my fellow graduates of the William S. Richardson School of Law (University of Hawai'i at Mānoa). Halfway through my remarks it began to rain—really hard, but only briefly. Afterward, one of my most beloved elders, Uncle Kekuni Blaisdell, came up to tell me that the rain was a blessing, that my mana (or power) was strong, and that he loved me. I cherish that day for many reasons, but most of all for the twin blessings of rain and elder.

Despite what we've been told, the world is not ours for the taking.

Indeed, the world we have inherited comes to us bruised, a tender shard of its former self, having passed clumsily through the well-intentioned hands of our mothers and fathers, seeking a generation it can trust enough, and long enough, to drop its shoulders.

Of the belief that love can save the world, I have a story to tell:

> *In the old days in the land now known as Guam, when the people lost their connection to their way, when the rains would not come and the people grew wild with hunger, a giant fish determined to destroy Guam began to eat the*

island widthwise, one giant chunk after another. Day after day, the men of Guam tried to stop it. They pursued it with spears, tried in vain to trap it, to catch it with nets they had made. They called upon the ancestors to aid in the capture. Every day, the women of Guam offered to help catch the giant fish, and every day the men, forgetting the strength of women, rejected them.

One night, while the women were weaving the pandanus leaves, the answer came to the maga'håga, the elder and leader among them. The women would weave a giant net from their long black hair. One by one, the women, old and young, came forward, knelt on the black stone, and parted with their beauty. Then they got to work, weaving and chanting through the night. By first light, they finished the net and set the trap. Though the giant fish convulsed violently, it could not break the net. Imbued with the women's intention, it was woven with deep spiritual affection and was therefore unbreakable. However, the women could not haul the giant fish ashore alone. When the men heard what was happening, they rushed to help the women and, together, they hauled the fish ashore. Its meat was shared with everyone.

It was our women's offering of beauty that saved Guam.

It has taken me many years to understand what this story is about, and why it is still passed down so many millennia later. I am convinced that its lessons, which have served my own people well, may be of some use to us today, as we look out at a world whose contours give us pause and make us feel at times as if whatever we do, whatever we are, will not be enough.

But, and here's the first lesson, no offering is too small. No stone unneeded. All of us—whether we choose to become human rights lawyers or corporate counsel, or choose never to practice law at all but instead become professors or entrepreneurs or disappear anonymous among the poor or stay at home and raise bright, delicious children—all of us, without exception, are qualified to participate in the rescue of the world.

But this is a quiet truth, and quiet truths are hard to hear when the cynics are outside howling.

Like the women who wove their hair into a magic net, we also do well to remember that saving the world requires all of our *hands*. As a group that has largely chosen the life of the mind, this will be especially important to remember. It would be a great folly to think that our ideas, no matter how good, would be enough to reverse the dangerous, downward trajectory of our planet. As an activist on the ground, I have often suspected that it is harder for people to rush to the rescue of a world whose magic they have not encountered for themselves, have not seen, felt, touched, turned over in their own hands. I for one can say without pause that so large a part of my own devotion to the cause of justice is that I have hiked up my pants and stood in other peoples' rivers. Moved to their music. Carried their babies. Watched them come back from burying their dead.

Our next lesson is that any people who profess to love freedom permit others room. Room to grow, to change their minds, to mess up, to leave, to come back in. In our story, the women did not reject the men who had done the same to them. They accepted their help, welcomed it. True, they could not haul in the fish alone, and needed the men. But perhaps that is the whole unromantic, utterly useful point: the part cannot save the whole. And I think this should not so much make us tentative, as it should anchor us in the reality of our collective vulnerability, in the immediacy of our connection.

So anchored, another truth becomes plain: it is strength, not power, that must be the object of our affection.

Finally, a word about beauty:

I have been thinking about beauty so much lately. About folks being robbed of it, folks fading for want of it, folks rushing to embrace only ghosts of it.

There have been periods in my own life when my grief felt more real to me than my hope, moments when my rage, sitting up, threatened to swallow my softness forever. It is here, in these moments, in these fields where older versions of myself come to die, that I am forced again to clarify what exactly it is that I believe. For example, though so much of my energy of late has been in the service of opposing the largest military buildup in recent history, which is now underway in my homeland, I don't really believe that I am, that we are, going to stop the US Defense Department from doing what it will. So what is it that I, that we, believe really?

In law school, we are taught early on the importance of keeping it tight. We learn to revere the elegance of restraint.

We become tailors who sew beautiful clothes of our reason. Somewhere along the way, we pick up a reflex. An intuitive feeling that we should only fight the fights we can win. Lawyer inside the narrowest possible nook.

But this is not *our* way. As lawyers fashioned in the Richardson tradition, these are not the only tools in our toolkit. In our hands, we hold a precious version, passed carefully to us by our teachers, of what it means to be a lawyer, of how it looks to begin cool from the premise that the law is not neutral, and then thoughtfully, strategically, politically go about using it in the service of justice.[7]

This is what I love most about Richardson. If we paid attention, even to the silences, we leave here knowing that it is not good enough just to go out and fight the fights we can win. Rather, Richardson nurtures in us a respect for possibilities, and when we are ready, gently says to us, even without saying it, go out and fight the fights that need fighting.

In the relay, something else, something so quiet it can barely be heard, is also transmitted. Let us look at it in the light. Each of us who decides to engage in social change lawyering must find our own way to build an inner life against the possibility, and a certain measure of inevitability, of failure.

---

[7] I'd be remiss if I didn't clarify that not everyone shares this view of Richardson. Like any law school, Richardson has its lot of establishmentarian professors, who seek to serve, not subvert, the status quo. Also, unlike some other law schools, Richardson has no formalized home for critical race studies. That said, certain faculty members go above and beyond to fill this institutional gap, providing a home for their progressive students. The Ka Huli Ao Center for Excellence in Native Hawaiian Law was that home for me. Particularly for the activist-turned-law-student, who knows very well that the law is not neutral because it is always already a moving train, having such a home is like having a life raft on a choppy sea.

Indeed, part of our work as people who dare to believe we can save the world is to prepare our wills to withstand some losing, so that we may lose and still set out again, anyhow.

I for one, especially of late, feel like I'm at a funeral when I go home. I see her: Guam, as a fishbowl for so many different kinds of dying. As many of you know, while here with you, I've been there, too. My focus always split. Three years later, I can tell you: the pipes of everything I've wanted desperately to stop are being fitted and laid. Despite how wide our movement has grown, and how fiercely articulate the generation rising to challenge the changing tide, we are losing.

But then, if I am quiet enough, I hear them, trooping in: the women who taught me how to go about this business of keeping on keeping on. I hear them, all the sounds that saved my life: my mother's bamboo bracelets, back and forth on the kitchen counter, as she, after hours on her feet, gets dinner ready; the hooks on the bottom of my grandmother's net, dragging on the floor, as she comes back fishless from the sea; the steady hooves of Cec's[8] horse, as she rides into the evening on the back of the only god she has left.

Having come from a tradition of beauty, of women's strength, of knowing what is worth wrapping one's arms around, I realize now that the most cherished of all things I am taking with me in the new morning is, quite simply, other people.

---

[8]There are so many women who have guided me throughout my life; Cec, or Cecelia Sheoships—a Cayuse-Umatilla woman whose love of horses is BEYOND—is one of them. More than anyone I've ever met, Cec embodies Rumi's call to, "[b]e a lamp, or a lifeboat, or a ladder. Help someone's soul heal. Walk out of your house like a shepherd."

Good morning to you all. What I wish for you is that, whatever work you do, be, as they say, your love made visible. That, and for your inner life, a good coat, because it can get very cold.

My mother, Annabelle, in our old house in Tumon, Guam

Sherman Alexie Looked
Me Dead in the Eye Once

Sherman Alexie looked me dead in the eye once.
At Auntie's Bookstore in Spokane. At the corner of
　　Washington and Main.
He was signing books when it happened.

I walk up to him with all the swagger of a shy
　　teenager.
And he knows what I'm going to say before
　　I say it.
I say I want to be a writer.
Sherman smirks and says, kid, tell me something I
　　don't already know.
Me: How could you possibly know that?
Him: I see it in your eyes, clear as day.
And right there, in Auntie's fiction section, I learned
　　something true about power.
That even small things like eyes can wield it.

Having been seen, I feel freed to testify.
I tell him I learned to read by his books.
As in *really* read. As in *disappear*.
I tell him *Reservation Blues* ruined me.

In the best possible way one could be ruined, which is
    to say, by art.
I tell him how hard I rooted for Thomas
    Builds-the-Fire.
To play the shit out of that magic guitar.
So his people could live.
How I rooted too for Robert Johnson.
To make it up Wellpinit Mountain.
So Big Mom could save him.
So he'd sing like her other horses.

I want to tell him so much more.
I want to thank him for leading me to other
    lighthouses.
To Louise's love medicine.[9]
To Joy's famous kitchen table.[10]
I want to thank him for writing wide.
As wide as a sea my own people can swim in.
My people, who are beautiful like his.

But I am nineteen and not sure.
And my words are not there when I reach for them.

---

[9]Louise Erdrich's beautiful book by that title meant so much to me when I was young. It was the first book to show me (not tell me) what the great writer John Berger meant when he wrote, "Never again will a single story be told as though it were the only one." Also, I had it in my head that Louise (in real life) must be kind, because only a kind person writes a book where no single voice or point of view dominates any other.

[10]I'm referring here to Joy Harjo's classic poem "Perhaps the World Ends Here," which is a glorious celebration of the kitchen table. As a Chamorro boy born and raised in Guam, however, I always secretly read the word "outside" into Joy's kitchen references, because where I'm from all the richness of life that she describes in the poem would invariably happen in our outside, not inside, kitchens.

So I smile and say nothing.

I turn and walk away, dragging my wordlessness with me, out into the busy street.[11]

---

[11]It took me longer to decide whether to include this piece than it did to write it. Like other Indigenous womanist writers, I remain troubled by the #MeToo allegations against Alexie, particularly the accounts of Native women writers who have described him as a cultural gatekeeper who abused his power and denied them passage. At the same time, as a youth inspired by his work, I'm still processing my grief, still sitting with my unresolved questions about how to continue to honor the impact his work has made without betraying his victims and survivors more generally. I made the difficult decision to include this piece because it is not fundamentally about Alexie at all, but about me and a formative moment in my life when I was young and yearning to see my own potential reflected back from an elder I admired.

More Right

MY AUNT LOU told me once that it is easier for our people to believe in magic than it is for others.

As soon as she said it, I knew it was true.

I knew because that day she'd taken my sister and me, plus two of our cousins, to a beach on the northern coast of the island where the sand is shaped like stars.

We got lost in those stars.

We bent over their tiny bodies for hours, inspecting them as closely as we could without a magnifying glass, wishing we had one, even if only one, even if it meant we had to share.

We made starcastles. We cartwheeled over constellations. We ran around and fell down on a blanket of stars. We took turns burying each other in a beautiful graveyard of celestial bodies.

My aunt's husband—a white man from Australia—explained later that they weren't stars at all but rather foraminifera—tiny single-celled creatures who live at the bottom of the sea, whose exoskeletons wash ashore when they die. Foram sands, he said.

He was right, of course, but my aunt was more right.

Because eyes wide with wonder is a perfectly good definition of magic.

Because magic could just as easily mean stargazing, in the midday sun, while looking down.

Because we had so little, yet somehow, we had it all.

Birthday Cakes Mean Birthdays

I wrote this op-ed for In These Times *in August 2017, when North Korea was threatening to bomb Guam and major media outlets descended on our small island for about a week. Since its publication, tension in the region has continued, with the United States ramping up its militarization of our lands and seas (including large-scale, multi-country war games). In August 2020, China launched four ballistic missiles into the South China Sea, one of which, the DF-26, it nicknamed "Guam Killer." While some in our community refuse to admit it, we are in danger no matter which country is flexing its military muscle in this tense geopolitical theater.*

Escalating tensions between the United States and North Korea culminated last week in increasingly specific threats to the island and people of Guam. North Korea announced that Guam was within striking range, and that it was "seriously examining" a plan to launch four intermediate-range ballistic rockets toward the island. One headline read, "14 Minutes," which is the amount of time they say it will take for a missile to reach us.

Fourteen minutes. To run for cover. Round up our children. Reach Deep.

Steel ourselves for the possibility of oblivion.

We need not worry, our leaders tell us. We are a resilient people. We need only summon that strength now. Will someone please tell them that resilience is not a thing to be trotted out in trying times like a kind of prized pony? As the gifted Haitian American writer Edwidge Danticat puts it, just because a people are resilient doesn't mean they can suffer more than others.

President Trump even phoned the governor of Guam, telling him that he, that the country, was "with [us] a thousand percent." The conversation devolved from there, with our governor, in a kind of curtsy, saying, "Mr. President . . . I have never felt more safe or so confident [than] with you at the helm . . . We need a president like you." The call lasted all of three minutes, with the two going on to talk about the local hotel occupancy rate, and the prospect of tourism going up "tenfold."

Mortifying though it was, it was also oddly intimate. Pillow Talkish.

For its part, Guam Homeland Security released a fact sheet of suggestions on how to prepare for an imminent missile threat—"Take cover behind anything that might offer protection," and "Lie flat on the ground and cover your head." And this one, for those of us unfortunate enough to find ourselves outside during the blast—"Wash your hair with shampoo, or soap and water. Do not use conditioner . . . because it will bind radioactive material to your hair."

What are we to do with these spectacularly useless suggestions? How can we not be defeated by this kind of extreme stupidity? Why is no one talking about the fact that nuclear war is unlike any other kind of war?

Last Wednesday, GOP Senator Lindsey Graham, in an interview with CBS This Morning, assured the American people that even if the Trump administration elects to go to war with North Korea, they should fret not, because at the very least, "if there's going to be a war, it's going to be in the region, not here in America."

And there it is. The Kiss of Kissinger.

From 1946 to 1958, the United States conducted an intensive nuclear testing program just 1,200 miles from Guam, in the Marshall Islands, where it detonated 67 atomic and thermonuclear weapons. Of these, a 15-megaton device known as "Bravo" was the worst. Detonated on March 1, 1954, it deposited life-threatening quantities of radioactive fallout on the Marshallese—some three times the estimated external dose to which the most heavily exposed people living near the 1986 Chernobyl nuclear accident were exposed.

They say the radioactive fallout was so thick that many Marshallese, having never seen snow, thought it was snowing. Children played in it.

It goes without saying that the nuclear testing program visited unspeakable violence on the Marshallese. The rate of miscarriages in the wake of these tests, for instance, is without parallel. One woman, a dear friend who has long since passed, suffered seven miscarriages in her lifetime. And this is to say nothing of the birth abnormalities that forced Marshallese women to have to devise an entirely new language to describe the things they've seen and the babies they've birthed—for example, jellyfish babies, or babies born without bones and translucent skin.

About this program, former National Security Advisor and Secretary of State Henry Kissinger had this to say:

"There are only 90,000 people out there. Who gives a damn?"

If US–North Korea relations be complex, this be simple: when you live in a colony, you're easy meat. That was Senator Graham's entire—and utterly unoriginal—point.

But alas the dogs have been called off.

The other day, the *Wall Street Journal* broke the story that the threat to Guam is gone. Jonathan Cheng, writing for the *Journal*, assured us that North Korea has "decided not to launch a threatened missile attack on Guam." But, Kim Jong Un warned, North Korea would still consider a strike if "the Yankees persist in their extremely dangerous reckless actions."

The other news outlets quickly followed suit, and, in the span of a few short hours, the weather had changed and the world had moved on. Reporters returned to their hotel rooms, sorted their suitcases, and booked their respective flights home.

They may have made their flights, but they missed the boat.

The truth is this. Nuclear weapons do not have to be used to be deadly. As Arundhati Roy says, it would be supreme folly to think so. "Nuclear weapons pervade our thinking. . . . They bury themselves like meat hooks deep in the base of our brains. . . . They are the ultimate colonizer."

Truer words were never written.

It was my partner's birthday on Sunday. It was mid-afternoon. I was headed to the nearby bakery to pick up a birthday cake. I was frustrated because I couldn't figure out where to put the cake once I picked it up, as my car was already full from the shopping I had done earlier that day. I had decided the day before that it was better to be safe than sorry, and so that morning I went out and bought two weeks' worth of supplies—canned food, powdered milk, a battery-powered radio. You know. Just in case. I was fussing with the bags in the back seat when it hit.

Birthday cakes mean birthdays.

Another year in the life of a loved one.

LIFE.

Guam may have to bear the burden of being a colony in a world suffering from decolonization fatigue, but—to be clear—her people mean to live.

Yugu Means Yoke

THE LAST THING I said to my father when he was still alive was how much I hated him for having cancer. And I hated him hardest the night before he died.

It was Halloween. I was a Teenage Mutant Ninja Turtle (Donatello), and all I wanted in the world was to get as far away from that hospital as I could. The hospital that smelled like spite and served as a second home to my siblings and me in the months leading up to his death.

I threw an epic fit after being told my chances of going trick-or-treating weren't good. I fretted as the hours rolled by, convinced there'd be no candy left by the time I got there. I let every adult in my dad's hospital room, including my dad, know how much I hated being there, hated cancer, hated him. I nagged my poor mother so hard she finally relented and told my oldest brother and his wife, who had just flown in from the States, to take my sister and me to the mall. I knew the candy there wouldn't be half as good as the candy from the houses in Nimitz Hill, but I was dying to get out of there, dying to breathe some other air, dying to have just a little bit of fun.

But of course, it was my dad who was dying.

Unbeknownst to me, he had been rapidly declining all that day and was, according to the doctors, decidedly on his way out of the world. Of course, I understood none of this then. At nine, one cannot read the signs—cannot see the harried pacing of nurses for what it is, cannot see the emptiness in a soon-to-be widow's eyes.

After we buried him, we moved permanently into the house on the hill. The blue-and-white house on the highest hill in Mount Santa Rosa. The house where everything rusted from the saltwater winds that blew in with a vengeance from the Philippine Sea. The house that was never a home.

I hated that house. So did my sister. I suspect my brother did, too, though he never said so. It's hard to tell because we barely spoke at the time, at least not about anything that mattered. In fact, I mostly avoided him. In fact, we mostly avoided each other. Each of us mourned in our own way— my mom by crying, my sister by self-isolating, my brother by leaving, and me by eating. Believe it or not, though, that wasn't even the problem. The problem, as I see it now, was that each of us mourned *alone*—as opposed to *together*.

I see us so clearly. Each of us an island. All of us at sea.

We didn't stand a chance.

Luckily, we each found something to get us through those deeply lonely years—my mom found she could disappear into her work; my brother found a girlfriend; my sister found Janet Jackson and a bunch of our dad's old shirts, which she wore religiously because she smelled him in them; and I found a whole wide world on that red-dirt mountain.

The first thing I found was a family of tree snails, which I'd spend hours watching, wondering why they moved so slowly, wondering if they could, if they had to, move swiftly enough to save their own lives. I found so many things after that. I found I could slide down the smaller slopes at the back of my house if I had just the right piece of cardboard. I found out the hard way that before one runs through an open field of sword grass, one should wear a long-sleeved shirt. I found no need for a bike. I found butterflies in abundance. I found more grasshoppers than I could count. I studied them closely, that is, when they'd let me get close. I was awed by how far their little legs could take them. I couldn't for the life of me fathom how such small legs could support such big hops. I wondered endlessly about wings. I was envious of everything that could fly. I prayed, without knowing how to, for wings of my own.

I wasn't the only one.

Further down the dirt road, my friend hanged himself in his house. The house closest to the bus stop where we took the bus to school every day. The house where words were shouted not spoken. The house that was never a home.

I learned so many things after that. I learned that same friend was an artist. That he loved to draw. That he drew a picture of a friend just before he died. That he tucked it away in a box beneath his bed. That he was capable of gentleness. I did not exactly know that because my friend was also, sometimes, my bully. But that's the other thing I learned. That when we are in pain, we inflict pain. That when we feel we can no longer breathe, we grab other peoples' air.

I also learned this: Yigo, the village we lived in, comes from the Chamorro word yugu.

Yugu means yoke. As in to bear a heaviness or to carry a burden.

We all bore that heaviness.

My sister most of all.

I know this because once when I was ten and she was eleven, I found her outside in the middle of the night, wearing nothing but my dad's old shirt, which she had washed one too many times and which, she said, no longer smelled like him. Though it had been only one year since he died, I was beginning to be able to read the signs. I could see the emptiness in her eyes.

I changed my prayer right then and there.

I prayed for her wings, not mine.

The only picture I have of my sister Rhea from 1992, the year after our father died, where she's smiling. It is one of my most precious possessions.

A Crowbar and a Conch Shell

Quiet as it's kept—[12]
I have always loved Epeli[13]
most. The erudite
irreverent
father of
all of
Oceania

who emerged
fully formed
from the sea
with a crowbar
and a conch
shell—

---

[12]From the famous opening lines of Toni Morrison's debut novel, *The Bluest Eye* ("Quiet as it's kept, there were no marigolds in the fall of 1941."). There is little left to say about Toni than what has already been said by countless others before me, but I'll say this: if there were ever such a thing as the Great American Novel, *Beloved* would almost certainly be it.
[13]I'm referring here to Oceania's most beloved public intellectual, Epeli Hau'ofa. I love Epeli for many reasons, including his genius and his wicked sense of humor, but one of them has to be because he wrote one of my all-time favorite books, *Tales of the Tikongs*. The first time I read it, I was on a flight to Fiji. By the time I got to the glorious scene where Manu is finally proven right and mounts his bicycle with gleeful abandon—and a placard reading, "DEVELOPMENT IS A LIE, TIKO KNOWS SWEET BUGGER ALL, AUSTRALIAN COWS ARE QUEER AND NEW ZEALAND BULLS CAN'T DO NO DAMN GOOD EITHER"—I was so overcome with delight I accidentally threw the book at the back of another passenger's head and damn near peed my pants!

the one to
worry loose
every locked
door in our
beautiful
blue
house

the other to
blare through the
night to call
every last
one of his
children
home.

Like Toni,
Epeli

spun gold
from pain

loved us
always a
little
more
than we
deserved

and
knew
above
all

the things
underneath
the things

knew

the function of
freedom is to
free
somebody

else.[14]

---

[14]From Toni's 1979 Barnard College commencement speech.

The Gift Anne Gave Me

APART FROM a few singing contests, the earliest thing in life I can remember winning was a Congressional Award. This was a citizenship award given to one graduating senior in each of Guam's high schools, who, in addition to academic excellence, showed a strong commitment to a life of civic engagement.

I vaguely recall Robert Underwood, Guam's congressman at the time, handing me a wooden plaque. What I recall more vividly is the rush of well-meaning adults who came up to congratulate me and, incidentally, tell me I already had their vote should I ever decide to run for office. A future, they took pains to tell me, they could clearly foresee.

It struck me that day how long we've labored under the misunderstanding that civic engagement and electoral politics are one and the same; how completely we've conflated leadership with elections. No wonder most of our history books are teeming with the ghosts of dead politicians; we've filled their pages with so many former governors, senators, and speakers of the house, it's no surprise no one else fits.

We've paid dearly for this mistake of history. We've paid in children whose growth was unnecessarily stunted. We've paid in ancestors whose names we do not know and thus cannot call out in times of tribulation—loved ones lost to us forever.

But sometimes they are found.

I found mine in a tiny classroom on the third floor of the humanities building at the University of Guam, while attending a lecture by Professor Anne Perez Hattori.

Anne, whose scholarship centers on the history of the US Naval Administration's colonial rule of Guam, was presenting her research on the leper colony that had been established by the navy in the early 1900s. Chamorros afflicted (or thought to be afflicted) with Hansen's Disease had been quarantined on a beach in the village of Tumon.

As part of her research, Anne spent a good deal of time in the National Archives. There she stumbled upon a 1912 article in the *United States Naval Medical Bulletin*, written by Navy Assistant Surgeon Dr. W. M. Kerr, which described the physical manifestations of leprosy among patients from Guam.

The article contains the only known individual photographs of the leprosy patients who were thought to be lost forever when the military government forcibly deported them from Tumon to the Culion Leper Colony in the Philippines in 1912.

The images are disturbing, like so much of the medical photography of that era, because they surreally reflect the dehumanization of their subjects. To be sure, the navy had replaced the names of these fifteen men and six women with numbers. The photographs, which bear only the subject's initials and corresponding case number, show these individuals in varying stages of undress, many of them nude, posed so that their affected body parts are displayed.

These photos were locked away for years in a filing cabinet in Anne's office, as she wrestled with the question of whether releasing them for public consumption would make her a collaborator in the crimes committed against these people. After several years of soul-searching, she finally released them, thereby starting several families down the long road toward healing.

The photo that changed my life was the last one she showed that day—a photo of two people who had escaped the colony the night before they were to be shipped off to Culion.

The first was a woman, known only by the initials JQT, who could not walk. The second was a man, known only by the initials LRR, who could not see.

Together, against all odds, the two managed to escape.

The one carrying the other. The one the other's eyes.

I nearly broke in half looking up at their brave faces.

As a young activist who had never felt more at home than in the struggle for social justice, and who had always longed to inherit a more magical legacy than the one on offer, the gift Anne gave me was nothing less than the ancestors I had looked for my whole life. Ancestors I could count on. Ancestors I could claim.[15]

---

[15]Of course I don't mean this in an exclusive sense, as there are many ancestors (lineal and not) whose legacies light my way, including: Hurao, our fiercest chief, who didn't take shit lying down, who believed in us more than we believed in ourselves; Auntie Henrietta, my great-aunt and one of Guam's first trans women who was ahead of her time in every way; JD Crutch, who was born to sing, whose music, when combined with a steady rain, can break absolutely anybody's heart; and Auntie Katchang, who always welcomed me warmly into her Agana Heights home and always, without fail, offered me something to drink. My point is simple enough: let's get off this boring ride of endlessly valorizing politicians.

Years later, Anne would tell me that naval officers at the time were not only baffled—as to how these two managed to pull off what might be the most implausible escape in history—they were also chafed because the pair was able to hide in the jungle for a whole month despite the navy's reward of fifty dollars each for their capture.

I smiled so wide when she said this.

Out of sheer fucking pride.

JQT and LRR, my ancestors whose escape from the leper colony in Tumon will go down in history even though their names may not.

Nirmal Hriday

THE SUMMER I turned nineteen, I lived along the banks of the Yamuna River.

In a Tibetan refugee camp called Majnu-ka-Tilla, which sprang to life in the 1950s after China invaded Tibet and the Indian government provisionally welcomed His Holiness the 14th Dalai Lama and his people.

Every day I walked to work by crossing the bustling street that separated Little Tibet from the rest of the world.

I worked for Mother Teresa at her Home for the Dying and Destitute.

A home where I said prayers at sunrise and swept and mopped the floors; where I changed bedding and bandages for bedsores; where I served hundreds of meals of rice and daal.

A home where I learned that the first step to growing a global heart is letting it break into hundreds of pieces. That summer my own heart broke in several directions at once.

It broke for all the foreseeable reasons—the grinding poverty, the insistent legacy of caste, the encircling despair—but it broke for all the unforeseeable ones, too.

It broke, for instance, with the burden of unrequited questions.

For all the pain I saw in that Delhi compound, day in and day out, where were the painkillers? More importantly, where were the nurses? The doctors? Why did I not once see one of them? Was it appropriate for an eighteen-year-old with zero experience and exactly ten minutes of training to be dressing wounds? Why did the sisters—of Mother Teresa's order, the Missionaries of Charity—abruptly rebuff even the most innocent questions put to them by my fellow volunteers and me, swatting at them like an annoying family of flies? Why was there talk only of love and never of justice?

The thought that the late British American journalist Christopher Hitchens could be right about the religious order worried me awake at night.[16] His exceedingly polemical nature aside, his question—whether the order was more interested in glorifying suffering than relieving it—was honest and had to be asked.

Being a transient teenage volunteer, however, I was hardly the person to ask it.

So, I did the only thing I could do. I packed up my uncertainties and went home.

It would be twenty years before those same uncertainties would come galloping back.

On a Tuesday morning in July 2018, while sitting quietly in my living room, I came across a story in the *Guardian* about a baby-selling scandal implicating the Missionaries of

---

[16]Though the well-known polemicist was not Mother Teresa's only critic, he was the most vociferous. His criticism can be found in his 1994 "Hell's Angel" documentary, which he produced with Tariq Ali, and his 1995 essay, "The Missionary Position: Mother Teresa in Theory and Practice."

Charity. One of the sisters had been arrested for selling a newborn for just over a thousand dollars. Together with a co-conspirator, Sister Konsalia Balsa confessed to having sold three babies before that, for roughly six hundred dollars each.

I sat stunned for a long while.

Later, I went foraging around for photos from that summer and found some.

One of them stood out. It was taken in late May, days before my nineteenth birthday.

Some of us had finished our work early and decided to gather the many orphaned children hanging around the compound to play.

And play we did. For hours. Tag. Dodgeball. Jump rope.

Even the sisters succumbed to the joy and joined in on the jump roping.

What I remember most about that day is every one of those children looking light—looking unburdened by the crushing poverty that brought them there; looking wondrously carefree, as all children, when they are not being crushed, should look.

Though I harbor doubt to this day—about my time there, about some of the order's methods, even about relief work in general, at least the kind that's divorced from any analysis of the causes of poverty—I have absolutely no doubt about what I saw that gorgeous May day.

I saw children who were clearly cared for. I saw the women who cared for them. I saw the trace of love's unmistakable signature.

Mother Teresa's Home for the Dying and Destitute, in Hindi, is called Nirmal Hriday.

The Home of the Pure Heart.

I don't know if hearts can ever really be pure.

They can, however, be good.

Mugo'

THEY SAY if you take the mugo' from a dog's eyes and rub it into your own you can see the dead.

They lied.

I know because I tried.

After dad died.

Rubbed more mugo' in my eyes than I care to admit.

And that's not the crazy thing.

The crazy thing is I didn't have a dog.

So, I settled for strays.

Chased those poor dogs all around the neighborhood.

Because beggars can't be choosers.

Because desperation, like belief, is a powerful thing.

And because I was Ten. And could not yet put Two and Two Together.

I somehow thought if I could see my dad, I could *speak* to him, too.

Ask him all my questions.

Do you like heaven? Are you and God friends?

Do you miss us?

Do you miss ME?

Do you still have a body? Is it chubby like before cancer or skinny like after?

What's your favorite food? Mine is cheese. Is yours? Is that because chä'ka—our family name on your side—means rat?

What about Aguon?

My teacher said Aguon refers to the family of tubers—as in taros and yams.

Why is "tuber" such a weird word?

And how are we related to taros and yams?

How EXACTLY?

Can you help Mom?

All she does is walk around sad and cry in that scary way where she shakes but don't make no sound.

Also she faints a lot. Also can you help Rhea?

She don't talk no more. She don't laugh.

It's too quiet in the house.

Can you come back and make it noisy again?

I chased those poor dogs for nothing.

I never saw him. Never got to ask him all my questions.

The medical term for mugo' is rheum. A fancy word for eye gunk. The crust that collects in the corners of our eyes, sometimes, after a good night's sleep. A natural part of healthy eye function, doctors say, nothing more.

But then doctors don't know everything.

The Ocean Within

I gave the following speech in May 2010 to the graduating class of Simon Sanchez High School—exactly ten years after graduating from that school myself. Though some of the details (such as the specific problems our community faced at the time) have changed, the larger message remains. The speech was published the next year by Storyboard, *a literary journal run by the University of Guam, and has been read by thousands of local high school and college students since.*

GRADUATES:

When I first thought of you, I was so happy to think of the adventures that await you. Soon some of you will pack up your bedrooms, board planes, and journey to cities like Seattle and San Francisco for college. Others will stay and pursue a degree at the University of Guam. Others still will join the workforce, enlist in a military branch, learn a trade. Some of you have absolutely no idea what you want to do. What you all have in common is that today marks the end of a chapter in your life—adolescence—and pretty soon, whether you're ready or not, the world will demand more from you.

In the coming years, you will be challenged in ways unfamiliar to you now. You will be forced to make some difficult decisions; defend what you believe. You will be prodded, pushed. Tested. You will be bumped up against the Great Wall of Uncertainty again and again—the question on the tongue of the universe always the same: *Who are you?*

So when I look out at you, I must admit my enthusiasm is tinged with concern. I worry because I know that by virtue of having come of age on this island, you may be in danger of not having what you'll need on your journey to adulthood.

Let me explain.

Growing up in Guam, we constantly hear the word "can't." We are always hearing about what we don't have, what is not possible, what can't change. We become fluent in the language of limitation. Just read the news. The message we constantly get is some variant of this: Guam's broken. Probably unfixable. The Guam Memorial Hospital is at capacity. All the beds are taken. Code Red. The Guam Department of Education is in trouble and may lose millions more in federal funding. Any minute now, the bottom will fall out. Take the popular local expression OOG, Only on Guam. We all know what this means. How can we be self-governing when we can barely cut paychecks by five o'clock on Friday? When we can't even close Ordot Dump? What I am talking about is fatalism. Fatalism is the idea that we are powerless to do anything to change our circumstances, to change the world. What does this mean? What does this look like? More importantly, what does this do to children?

I cannot think of anything more terrifying than children who do not believe the world can be changed. Children who do not dream, do not grow. They grow up, but they do not grow. Do not become adults. Adulthood is when we discover who we are. It's when we figure out some really important stuff—like what our strengths and weaknesses are, what our unique individual gifts are. Also, what shortcomings we must mitigate. It's when we go through that very important process of introspection, soul-searching, self-discovery. If we do not go through this process, we inevitably become unhappy people who wake up in the morning empty, afraid, unfulfilled.

Guam is a microcosm of the world. It is confused and suffering. And it needs you desperately. It needs more hospital beds, yes. More doctors, in fact. More teachers, more environmentalists, more social workers. More farmers and fisherfolk, too. Guam needs all these things. But what this island really lacks—what it really, really needs—is more imagination. More dreaming.

In some ways our island, though surrounded by water, is a desert—a desert of imagination. So many in our community have an impression, a sense, that they are not smart enough or capable enough to do things, not monied enough to travel, not talented enough to make a living from their art. So many of us so early on in life give up on our dreams. We place our dreams in boxes, seal them shut, and shelve them somewhere just out of sight. Maybe that's what colonialism looks like: Dreams Under Duct Tape.

There is a book, *The Alchemist*, that tells of the importance of quieting down the noise of the outside world, the noise of other people, and listening instead to one's own heart. The book is about a young shepherd boy who journeys to the deserts of Egypt in search of a treasure he has dreamed about.

Along the way, the boy faces many challenges and, at one point, finds himself penniless in a foreign land. He eventually gets a job in a small crystal shop, where he learns about the danger of abandoning one's dreams from the shop owner, who himself lacked the courage to go in search of his dreams and, as a result, lived a life of emptiness. The boy eventually reaches the desert, where he slowly starts to learn what is described in the book as the "Language of the World." In the desert, the boy gets quiet, learns to read the omens and, finally, listens to his heart. In the end, he learns that one's only real obligation is to realize one's destiny.

What I want to tell you today is this: Get quiet. In each of you, there is a whisper that speaks of a special, unduplicated gift that you alone possess and are meant to bring forth into the world. Attend to that whisper. Jesus said: "If you bring forth what is within you, what is within you will save you. If you do not bring forth what is within you, what is within you will destroy you." I dare to add—if you bring forth what is within you, what is within you will save other people, too.

When we do what we love, we nourish the soul of the world. When we do something else, something we don't love, we run the risk not only of being very unhappy people, but of hurting other people as well, even people we supposedly love. In fact, we run the risk of never knowing love at all; that is, the kind of love that is separate from possession. If we don't learn how to be quiet and attend to that whisper in each of us, if we fail to cultivate our own inner gift, we grow cold. Less kind. Quick to rush to blot out other people's light. You might know this phenomenon as the crabs-in-a-bucket syndrome. We in Guam have had enough of that.

I originally intended to buy each of you a copy of *The Alchemist*. Long story short, I couldn't swing it. I do, however, have something for you. With your programs, you'll find a seashell. This shell is special. It was not imported from somewhere else; not bought from any store. Local artists have spent the last several weeks combing the beaches, retrieving them for you.

There is a beautiful exchange in the book between the alchemist and the boy after days of traveling the desert. The alchemist was explaining to the boy why it is that some people who set out to be alchemists are never able to turn the other metals into gold. He told the boy that those who are interested only in gold do not understand the secret of alchemy. In their singular obsession, they forget that lead, copper, and iron all have their own destinies to fulfill. And anyone who interferes with another's destiny will never discover their own. So, the alchemist reached down and picked up a shell from the ground. "This desert was once a sea," he said. The alchemist told the boy to place the shell over his ear. "The sea has lived on in this shell, because that's its destiny. And it will never cease doing so until the desert is once again covered by water."

Graduates, at the beginning of my talk, I told you that I worry you may be in danger of not having what you'll need on your journey to adulthood. These small shells are my attempt to equip you. May they remind you of the ocean within you—your destiny. When the world gets noisy—and it will—remember them. Get quiet.

If you would, please place your shells over your ears.

If you can learn to be quiet, if you can become good listeners to your own ocean, you—and Guam—will be better for it.

We Have No Need for Scientists

We have no need
for scientists to
tell us things
we already
know
like the
sea is
rising
and the
water is
getting warm.

The inundated need no instruction in inundation.

We have eyes
of our own
and besides
we are busy
scraping
barnacles
off our grandfathers'
graves
and other

headstones
drowned
at high
tide.

We know
how critical
it is our
coral reefs
stay healthy
and our
mangrove
forests
dense.

We will
defend
them
to the
end
not because
some study
shows they
provide
protection
from
erosion
or shelter
from

storms
but because
our reefs
are adoring
aunts
feeding
other
people's
children
and our
mangroves,
mothers
in their
own right.

We Reach for You[17]

WE REACH for you today as you gather in memory of this bloodiest of battles.

As you stand against our increasingly militarized world, demand justice, and shame the powerful with the depth of your courage and your love, know we are with you.

You who know that death is only one kind of dying.

You who light candles and line roadways and block trucks and boats with your bodies.

You who hold up more than your fair share of the sky. We reach for you.

We hold your faces in our hands.

[17]"We Reach for You" is a statement of solidarity delivered in June 2007 at the 62nd anniversary of the Battle of Okinawa.

Reflections While Driving[18]

I wrote this reflection in October 2019 on the eve of the deadline of the government of Guam's decision to appeal Davis v. Guam *to the Supreme Court of the United States (SCOTUS). I served as lead litigator in the case for nearly a decade, defending the ability of the native inhabitants of Guam to exercise our right of self-determination by way of a plebiscite regarding our future political relationship with the United States. This case is more important to me than any others I've argued—not only because self-determination is one of the most sacrosanct rights in all of international law, but also because an insidious trend has taken hold of the federal bench ever since SCOTUS handed down its problematic decision in* Rice v. Cayetano *in 2000. Since* Rice, *those of us Indigenous peoples living under US rule (but falling outside the state-centered framework of federally recognized Indian tribes) have had to fend off one constitutional attack after another, with few doctrinal tools left at our disposal.*

IT'S BEEN NEARLY ninety days since the Ninth Circuit handed down its decision in *Davis v. Guam*, affirming the grant of

---

[18] A title borrowed from the Swarthmore College admissions essay of one of my oldest friends, Seeta Sistla. Seeta, for whom curiosity is the highest virtue, is also the person who, when we were sixteen, compiled what remains the longest reading list of my life, with everything from Gabriel García Márquez's *One Hundred Years of Solitude* to Ken Kesey's *One Flew Over the Cuckoo's Nest*.

summary judgment in favor of Arnold "Dave" Davis on Fifteenth Amendment grounds.

In its 41-page decision, the panel tacitly acknowledged the injury of colonization, squarely rejected Davis's argument that ancestry is equivalent to race, and preserved our Fourteenth Amendment arguments regarding a compelling interest in advancing self-determination. Yet, we lost.

The decision marks the second time in history that a white plaintiff successfully invoked the protections of the Fifteenth Amendment to judicially invalidate a program designed to protect people whose homelands were, at one point in time, wrongfully acquired by the United States. The first was *Rice v. Cayetano*.

In *Rice*, the Supreme Court held that a state law that premises the right to vote for state officials on Native Hawaiian ancestry violates the race-neutrality command of the Fifteenth Amendment. The circumstances of that case are vastly different from a nonbinding expression of self-determination by a class of colonized people in an unincorporated territory—a territory which, by definition, is neither destined for statehood, nor considered bound in permanent union with the United States.

I believe the Supreme Court was incorrect to hold that the Hawai'i law was a racial classification, but the Court of Appeals was bound by its holding. Even so, *Rice* was a limited decision, and I believe the appeals court was wrong to extend its logic to Guam. Yet, it did. It rejected the faulty argument that ancestry-based classifications are always racial classifications, a holding that will no doubt help in challenges to Native American rights.[19]

Yet, as in *Rice*, the court held that a law limiting voting rights to colonized peoples and their descendants *is* a racial classification. For those of us colonized peoples who live outside the state-centered framework of Indian tribes, the courts still seem to believe that ancestry does equal race.

Rice and *Davis* (along with a third decision allowing non-native people to vote to repeal land laws in the Commonwealth of the Northern Mariana Islands) laid dangerous doctrinal groundwork. It will now be even harder for colonized peoples to exercise any measure of self-determination (at least where an act of voting is involved) because the mere act of designating who constitutes the colonized class could collapse, in a court's eyes, into an act of racial categorization. It will now be even more difficult to determine the collective desire of a colonized people because we cannot even name those people in order to ask them.

This should excite serious constitutional alarm, as the only real remaining import of the Insular Cases today is that they contemplate the ability of unincorporated territories to "break out" of the Union. Setting aside whatever legal mischief has been done in their name, the Insular Cases effectively smuggled a theory of secession into American law.[20]

---

[19] Law professor Addie Rolnick—one of my most trusted colleagues (and ride-or-dies)— provided invaluable counsel to me throughout the yearslong litigation, helping me unpack the many ways in which the legal doctrines undergirding Indian law and territorial law do (and do not) intersect. Those years would've been bitterly lonely without her. Erwin Chemerinsky and Linda Hamilton Krieger, with their cavernous minds, were also incredibly generous with their counsel.

[20] A line lifted from a 2010 interview of territorial law scholar Christina Duffy Ponsa-Kraus, entitled "Islands and the Law: An interview with Christina Duffy Burnett."

Despite this, I hesitate to use the word "disappointed" to describe how I feel about the decision. Disappointed is a lover's word, and we should stop using it—at least to describe the American legal system and the judgments it produces.

Not once since 1898—America's imperial meridian—has this country been able to come up with a satisfactory legal justification for maintaining its constellation of overseas colonial possessions—territories deemed not to be a *part* of the United States, but rather to *belong* to the United States. The constructive violence done to the text of the Constitution in the name of colonial enterprise is surpassed only by the real violence inflicted upon the psyches of folks who must find our way in a country that neither wants us nor wants to let us go.[21]

More than a hundred years have produced no resolution to this constitutional crisis except at the expense of the peoples of the territories, and the loss, to the world, of the gift of our difference.[22]

But this is not what I came here to say.

I wanted to say this: beyond the outcome in *Davis v. Guam*, beyond the question of whether or not to appeal the same—indeed, beyond ideas of winning and losing—there is a field.[23] A field of very real work to be done.

---

[21] A line inspired by Professor Ponsa-Kraus and her colleague, Burke Marshall, in their revealing book, *Foreign in a Domestic Sense: Puerto Rico, American Expansion, and the Constitution*.

[22] This sentence can be traced to the work of constitutional law scholar Milner Ball, albeit in the context of federal Indian law, in his seminal article, *Constitution, Court, Indian Tribes*.

[23] A line inspired by a Rumi poem that begins, "Out beyond ideas of wrongdoing and rightdoing, / there is a field. I'll meet you there."

The work of building community and building power; the work of interrupting the tired dynamic of always having to appeal to someone else, indeed our colonizer, to do something on our behalf; the work of creating the conditions whereby our people can live powerfully and live well.[24]

We can get there, but first we have to look up—look beyond the law's limited horizon. This is not to say that the law cannot deliver justice. Indeed, it does—but only on occasion, and rarely by design. As a system, it seeks to maximize order and predictability, not necessarily justice. Moreover, the law, especially American law, is limited in its power because harms like colonization, land dispossession, and racial subordination are woven into the very fabric of this country's being. As close to this country as a jugular vein.

We can get there, but first we have to know—way down deep in our moonpit[25]—that the imagination that got us into this mess will not be the one to get us out of it.

That we may be without a blueprint, but we are not without vision.

That what we love we can save—even ourselves, even each other, even when we are afraid.[26]

---

[24]This paragraph contains the powerful thoughts and ideas articulated by Black Lives Matter cofounder Alicia Garza over the course of multiple interviews.

[25]A line inspired by Audre Lorde's powerful poem, "The Black Unicorn."

[26]In May 2020, SCOTUS denied Guam's petition for certiorari. In August 2020, my firm, Blue Ocean Law, together with the Brussels-based Unrepresented Nations and Peoples Organization, filed a submission against the United States with the Special Rapporteur on the Rights of Indigenous Peoples (on behalf of community-based organization Prutehi Litekyan). In it, we detail the infringement of self-determination; free, prior, and informed consent; permanent sovereignty over natural resources; and other rights. Meanwhile, we continue to explore other international strategies in our broader pursuit of justice and redress.

Nikki and Me

I was in the ninth grade and on a bus on my way home from school.

Our usual bus driver—a bald man with sad eyes who we were convinced was having an affair because he listened to Mary MacGregor's 1976 hit, "Torn Between Two Lovers," every day like it was fresh—had taken time off, or so we'd assumed, because all of a sudden we had a new bus driver. Mr. Q.

A man with a full head of hair and mean eyes.

Mr. Q. hated Chuukese people.

We knew this because he made life a living hell for Xavier, or X, the one and only Chuukese boy on our bus.

Mr. Q. scolded X constantly and for no reason. Once he even yelled at him to "sit up straight," even though the whole bus was slouching. He mocked him. Made fun of his two gold teeth. Meted out punishments for nonexistent crimes.

One day, Mr. Q. handed one of my classmates—an emotionally disturbed boy whose parents were getting a divorce at the time—a pencil. A sharp one. Then he whispered something in his ear. Looked at X, then looked back. Whispered something else. Looked again, looked back.

We couldn't hear him, my friend Nikki and me, because we were too far back in the bus.

But we knew what was up. That pencil had a purpose. To stab. And X marked the spot.

Time stopped.

We look at each other nervously but say nothing. Look down at our shoes, then up at each other. Down. Up. Down. Nothing. Then, in a flash, we're up and out of our seats. Charging the front of the bus like a pair of raging baby bulls. No plan, nothing. Not a clue as to what we would do when we got there. Just two small stomachs turning over one thought: there was no way on earth we could live with ourselves if we just sat there. Silent. Staring at our shoes.

We got there in time, luckily.

We also got thrown off the bus.

Yup. Mr. Q. was a real bastard.

So we walked, Nikki and me, the whole way home.

More than three miles. Uphill. I can still feel the weight of my bag. I can still see it. Blue with a brown bottom.

But it's not the walking I remember, really. It's the talking.

We told each other things that day that neither one of us had the nerve to say before. I told her I liked boys. And that scared me. She told me she was almost raped. And that scared her. We talked about Ray—our friend who was the most beautiful boy in Mount Santa Rosa, who hanged himself just before school started. Before any of us could stop him. Before any of his dreams could come true.

Looking back now, everything about that day is so vivid, so clear. The bus, the boys, the pencil. The blue backpack with the brown bottom. But clearest of all is what I learned that day about what happens when we stand up for each other.

We find our friends. And our way home.

Onion and Garlic

I miss those days of
Tang-stained
fingers and
every kind of
fried rice

hide-and-
go-seek and
hula
hoop

red rubber
kickballs and
running in
and out of

cousins'
houses
and
corner
stores

for corned
beef and
coconut
milk

for
grandmothers

knife-wielding
women in
kitchens

with one eye
watching

for any
would-be
killers

calling on
our dreams
before their
time.

It is little wonder
onion and garlic
remind us
so much of
freedom.

Me, on my sixth birthday, when I lived in the village of Tamuning and the hula hoop was my jam.

Fighting Words

The following is a commencement address I gave in December 2018 to the graduating class of the University of Guam. Of all the speeches I've ever given, it is by far the most personal. For months afterward, perfect strangers cornered me in grocery stores and gas stations to let me know it helped them, if not to heal, then at least to face something.

WHEN I FIRST accepted the invitation to speak to you tonight, I knew only one thing for sure. I wanted to avoid the usual offerings that mark this occasion—the future is yours for the taking, don't be afraid to fail, risk big, dream bigger. One can trot out those prized ponies only so many times before they get a little long in the tooth. So I did what any good writer would do: I went in. I drew open the drawers of my own interior life and scanned their disheveled contents with an exacting eye. Memories and milestones and music albums. Books read and bread broken and battles won and lost. All the well-meaning and mean-spirited roadhouses on the road to understanding. I combed through all of it searching for something real, something more than a slogan, to share. For some small piece of useful truth I've learned about the world from having lived in it, on my own terms, as fully as I can.

I should warn you that what I'm about to share might be hard to hear. It is also quite graphic in its recounting of certain traumatic events, which might be a little much for a younger audience. But you are adults and you are moments away from walking off this stage and into the world as it actually is, not only as you wish it to be, so I'm going to go there.

There is a language heist afoot in this country[27] that is threatening our ability to show up for each other and for ourselves. We are losing our capacity to confront the injustice that is literally everywhere around us, and I think it has something to do with the kind of violence we are seeing today. In one sense, the violence raining down on the most vulnerable among us—immigrants, Indigenous peoples, asylum seekers, refugees, women, children—is horrifying, but it is not startling. Acts of violence against these and other groups are occurring with such frequency, news of it is not in fact new. Stories of thousands of children being separated from their parents, caged, and tear-gassed at the border. Stories of one unarmed black boy after another (after another) being shot dead by a murderous cop. These stories don't just come in with the morning paper. They come in with the morning light. These are stories of brutality, and they have become as banal

---

[27]I can appreciate that references to "this country," "we," and "our," throughout this piece may be a bit jarring, as it flies in the face of the fact that Guam is a colony—a possession as opposed to a part—of the United States. I am fully aware of that fact and, moreover, the endless ways the United States has stymied Chamorro self-determination efforts throughout history. That said, there are many in Guam, including many Chamorros, who not only feel loyalty to the United States but believe they are bona fide members of the American political family. Aware of this tension, I choose to honor it here, not hide from it, because language, like identity, is complex and there are times when it feels correct to be inclusive and to meet people where they actually are, even as we wage our various battles on the status quo.

as breakfast. Bacon and eggs. A cup of coffee. It is this banality of brutality that is truly troubling. One would think this enough to send us careening into collective action. But it's not, at least it hasn't been. I think part of the problem is that something else is happening, too. The violence that is everywhere erupting—at the borders of this country, in Waffle Houses in Georgia, in parking lots in Guam—is of a different degree. A man choked to death for selling loose cigarettes. A woman shot to death for burning white rice. What we are seeing in our communities is increasingly barbaric behavior. And it's immobilizing us, rendering us momentarily incapable of speaking—speaking back and speaking up.

One of my favorite writers, Alice Walker,[28] wrote a book about this phenomenon. Some years ago, while working with a women's antiwar group, she traveled to Rwanda, the eastern Congo, and Palestine, meeting with survivors of every conceivable kind of violence and listening closely to their accounts. In Rwanda, she recalls the racist origins of the genocide that rocked that country, culminating in the deaths of hundreds of thousands of Tutsis by the Hutu. She traces the story all the way back to the Belgians (and the Germans before that) who arrived on the scene after centuries of relatively peaceful coexistence between the two clans. So the Belgians decide that the Tutsi, because they had larger skulls, were more like Europeans and thus should be in charge of the Hutu (whose skulls, apparently, were not as large).

---

[28]Alice Walker's writing is like a meal prepared with love: deeply nourishing. Though she's most famous for her Pulitzer Prize-winning novel, *The Color Purple*, it is her nonfiction collection, *In Search of Our Mothers' Gardens: Womanist Prose*, that had the single greatest impact on me. I can't begin to describe what that work of art has meant to me.

They instigate this rule of one clan by the other, and it goes on like this for years. When they finally leave, the Belgians place the Tutsi in charge of the Hutu. Unsurprisingly, the hatred that had been building over such a long period erupted into the mass slaughter of 800,000 Tutsis. 800,000 Tutsis in 100 days.[29]

On her way to Palestine, while waiting at a border crossing in Rafah, a traveling companion hands Alice an illustrated postcard depicting a UN partition plan. On the back of the card are the words of former Israeli Prime Minister Ariel Sharon, known by many as the Butcher of Beirut, where he talks about making a pastrami sandwich of the Palestinian people, "riddling their lands with Jewish settlements until no one will be able to imagine a whole Palestine[,] [o]r know [it] ever existed."

Later, in the Gaza Strip, Alice sits in the rubble of recently bulldozed Palestinian homes. She learns of a woman (alive but unconscious) whose husband was killed during a twenty-two-day bombardment of Gaza, as were all five of her daughters. She wonders who will tell this woman this—when, or if, she wakes up. She wonders what language could possibly be up for the job. How do you tell a woman that her whole world has died?

Finally, in the eastern Congo, Alice meets with women who had been victims of rape on the scale of war crimes. One woman, who had been a sex slave for over a year until she escaped, talks about being raped with every imaginable

---

[29]This paragraph draws directly from a 2010 *Democracy Now!* interview with Alice Walker.

instrument, from the handle of a machete to the barrel of a gun. Others share similar stories. But one story shakes Alice Walker to her core. She writes:

The suffering had been unbearable as people were chased from their homes at all hours of the day or night; many of them choosing to sleep in the forest or hide themselves in their fields. [Generose] was home with her husband and two children because among other reasons, such as this was her home, her husband was sick. One evening, there was a fierce knock at the door, gunmen who also carried machetes entered, demanding food. There was little to offer them but the staple diet: a boiled vegetable . . . and a few balls of steamed millet. The men ate this, but were angry and not satisfied. They went and found the husband, still in bed, and hacked him to pieces on the spot. They came back to Generose and her children and took hold of her. Holding her down, they began to cut off her leg. They cut off her leg, cut it into six pieces, and began to fry it in a pan. When some part of it seemed nearly done, they tried to force her son to take a bite of it. Strongly, beautifully, and so much the son of our dreams, he said: No, I will never eat my mother's flesh. They shot him to death without more conversation. The daughter, seeing this, watching her mother bleeding to death, knowing her father had been hacked to pieces, was now offered the same opportunity. Terrorized, she bit into a piece of her mother's body. Her mother, having crawled away, does not know what became of her. Though she

does know that her assailants went next door that same
evening and murdered a couple who'd been married that
day, raping and mutilating the bride, and tearing out
her eyes . . . I have not forgotten this child who was
forced to eat her mother's flesh for a moment. Yet it has
been almost impossible to speak of it. Coming home I fell
ill with the burden of this story[.]

The book is called *Overcoming Speechlessness*.

When asked why she titled it that, Alice responded by saying that there are times when things are so horrible we literally lose the ability to talk about them. That is to say, in the face of suffering such as this—unspeakable suffering—we come undone. We are left bereft of words to bear witness. Constitutionally incapable of coming to anyone's rescue, including our own.

In the book, she is calling us to overcome that speechlessness. To push past it, to take a step beyond our trauma, and into the sun.

So here goes.

The first time I experienced this phenomenon was in the summer before fourth grade.

My family and I had been living in Portland, Oregon for two years, so that my mom could earn a master's degree in social work. Around the time she was finishing, my dad was diagnosed with pancreatic cancer. At the same time, my grandmother, who was suffering from early-onset dementia, was sent to Guam ahead of the rest of us, temporarily entrusted to a relative's care. One day, after my sister and I had returned home, we were taken to this same relative's house. What I saw that day would sit for years like a stopper in my throat.

Once at the house, we asked over and over again to see our grandmother, wondering why she was being kept from us. Some time passed. Then some more. After what seemed like an eternity, we heard a banging coming from a bedroom in the back. My uncle scurried away to attend to the noise. Unbeknownst to him, I had snuck quietly behind him. When he threw open the door, I saw her. My grandmother. Half-naked and tied to the bed. A brown rope. A silver bowl on the floor. Our eyes met. Hers were wild with fear. I froze. Then a slamming of a door. Then an uncle, with a smirk on his face, and a key (for a lock) in his hand. I must have passed out. The next thing I remember is my eight-year-old body hanging upside down by its ankles. Crying as two of my cousins passed me back and forth, laughing, knowing there was little I could do about it. Because I was little. And I had too little power. And I did not have the words with which to fight back, graft my rage onto the world, wage war. I had no command over the language I needed to set me, or her, free.

We would eventually get our grandmother out of that house, and she would spend several more years with us, into the evening of her life. Mine was the last face she would recognize, and the last name she would remember. My last act was singing to her, which incidentally was perfect form, as this was the same woman who played a mean harmonica and taught me to love music, the blues mostly, and bequeathed to me so many gifts (though of the spiritual and not the earthly kind) including an almost religious belief that if God had a voice, it would be Aretha Franklin's.

I've never shared any of this before. But I'm sharing it with you because I'm trying to be brave. And because, as a writer, this is my work to do. As the supremely gifted Arundhati Roy says, we are living in a time when our words have been butchered and bled of meaning.[30] We writers, then, are called. To take pail to water in this leaky boat of ours. To run toward, not from, our burning house. If not to rescue everyone, then to help as many people as possible rescue themselves, by rescuing back language itself. Back from the butcher.

These days I take pail to water mostly in my capacity as a human rights lawyer. Together with my team at Blue Ocean Law, we work both here at home and throughout the region, using the law to advance the rights and interests of island communities. We provide guidance to small island states trying to better protect their natural resources from outside exploitation. We help coastal communities challenge the multinational corporations aggressively seeking to mine the surrounding seabed, no matter the environmental or cultural cost. We go to court to defend the right of self-determination because the most categorically legitimate longing of human beings is the longing to be free.

---

[30]A line lifted from her powerful "Public Power in the Age of Empire" essay.

I share this because this is what it looks like when we are able to overcome our speechlessness, find our fighting words, and step into the sun.

We share the sunlight.

Graduates, if you look under your seats, you will find your own copy of *Overcoming Speechlessness*. I worked with the publisher (the good folks at Seven Stories Press in New York) and was able to buy each of you a copy. Lucky for me, they had exactly 273 copies left in their warehouse, which incidentally was exactly enough. Lucky for you, Alice Walker is among the most gifted of us. The kind of writer whose words are so powerful they are like ancestors—loved ones wishing to redeem us, to carry us closer to freedom, on their backs if need be. May you find not only your fighting words but your fighting spirit, too.

Our broken world is waiting.

My grandmother, Ana,
holding my mom.

Yeye Tere[31]

Yeye Tere

You who

confounded categories and
razed canons and
waged war
on the
General.[32]

You who
stained glass and
tempered steel and
forged metal
of your
students'
minds.

---

[31]"Yeye Tere" is dedicated to the late Oceanian scholar-writer-activist-queen Teresia Teaiwa.

[32]If there was one thing Teresia couldn't stand it was generalizations. She insisted on specificity in *everything*. Though she never said so, at least not to me, I suspect her insistence was rooted in something more than just an aversion to intellectual flabbiness; I think she thought that mutual respect, even love, demands we attend to detail in every possible way.

You who

made a
way

made
a bench for
children to
sit.

I trust you know
how many
of us
you

mothered

from the
milk
of your

beautiful
mind.

I trust you know we will
live,
as you
insisted,

on our own
terms.

Yeye Tere
(Mother Teresia)

I ran to the river
tonight

with a
basket of
seashells
plumerias (yellow)
and a fresh comb of
honey

an offering to
Oshun

so she'd fly
this prayer
to the
sun:

swim free.

Our Father

The following is a eulogy given in August 2017 for the great Marshallese statesman and global justice activist Tony de Brum—who, in life, was like a second father to me. A father I got to say goodbye to.

GOOD EVENING. I must start by saying it is an honor to be here with you to celebrate the life and legacy of one of the greatest men many of us have ever known: Uncle Tony de Brum.

Though I called him an uncle in life, he was more like a father to me, as he was to so many of us gathered here today.

I met our father about ten years ago. I was in Majuro doing research for a book I was writing at the time,[33] and he had generously agreed to sit and talk with me (as he'd done with hundreds of others before me and hundreds more after me). I remember it like it was yesterday. We were over at Tide Table Restaurant, at the Hotel Robert Reimers. We had lunch (fried fish), several cups of coffee, and even shared a slice of banana cream pie, which, I have to say, was rather good. Anyway, he patiently fielded a whole host of questions about the

---

[33] *What We Bury at Night* was a short collection of essays I wrote in the summer after my 1L year of law school, describing the experiences of many of us in Micronesia with US colonization and militarization.

devastating nuclear testing history here, and the ongoing struggle for reparations and redress. We talked for hours—well, he did most of the talking—about everything from the nuclear tests themselves[34] to the decades of nonconsensual experimentation that followed;[35] from his lifelong campaign for nuclear disarmament to his beautiful wife, Rosalie, their three daughters, and their near dozen grandchildren; from our shared love of sashimi to his unshakable belief that the best bigeye tuna in the world hails from here.

He told me many stories that day, but one of them shook the ground beneath my feet. He told me about the morning of March 1, 1954:

> *I was fishing for mackerel in the morning with my grandfather when the bomb was dropped. I was nine, but something like that you never forget. I was carrying the basket for my grandfather. I don't know how to describe it, but we knew immediately that something*

---

[34]It's difficult to describe the damage wrought by the 67 atomic and thermonuclear weapons detonated by the United States in the Marshall Islands. The following is a start: extensive radiological contamination of numerous atoll homelands, including, but not limited to, Enewetak, Bikini, Utrik, and Rongelap; decades-long (and, in some cases, ongoing) exile of several Marshallese groups due to residual radiation contamination in their home atolls; elevated incidences of congenital diseases, birth defects, miscarriages, and weakened immune systems; as well as high rates of thyroid, cervical, breast, and other cancers. And this is to say nothing of the devastating interruption to Marshallese cultural practices and the ability to transmit those same traditions to future generations.

[35]Though the public record is now replete with evidence substantiating this claim, it is the deeply dehumanizing way in which American scientists and doctors spoke of the Marshallese that always gutted me, and guts me still. For instance, one Dr. Merril Eisenbud had this to say at a 1956 meeting of the Atomic Energy Commission: "[I]t will be very interesting to go back and get good environmental data, so as to get a measure of the human uptake when people live in a contaminated environment . . . While it is true that these people do not live, I would say, the way Westerners do, civilized people, it is nevertheless also true that these people are more like us than the mice."

was wrong. We knew that tests were being done, bombs were being dropped. We had seen and heard some of them before. But this was different. Everything seemed to happen within a few seconds. It was not a boom. Atomic and hydrogen bombs don't do that. They don't boom. They rumble. Like thunder. The sky turned completely red. And this was about six o'clock in the morning. It was like someone had put me and my grandfather in a glass bowl and poured blood in it. The beach was red, the ocean was red, the fish in my basket was red. I peed in my pants. I grabbed my grandfather and he threw everything down and half-carried me back to the house. My aunt normally ran our household but she was not on Likiep at the time; she was on Majuro. My grandfather gave me and my cousin two pieces of rebar to go bang on the community bell, which was an oxygen tank hanging from a tree, calling everyone to the house. We were so confused. It was supposed to be daylight, but it was deep red, like blood.

I could not know then that this story would change the course of my life, or that this man, whose warm eyes gleamed with equal parts mischief and magic, would change the course of history itself—and not only for his own people, but for all of us. It would be about eight years before I would watch, along with the rest of the world, this same man become the driving force behind the High Ambition Coalition, which would secure global consensus in the eleventh hour of the 21st Conference of the Parties, resulting in the Paris

Agreement and giving Pacific Islanders everywhere a fighting chance. You know: 1.5 to stay alive.[36]

Thankfully, our father's contributions to the global struggles for nuclear and climate justice were recognized in real time, as evidenced not only by his Right Livelihood Award (a.k.a. the Alternative Nobel Peace Prize)—and later his nomination for the *actual* Nobel Peace Prize—but also by the glowing tribute that the editorial staff of the *New York Times* recently wrote in his honor.

I was fortunate enough to spend some time with our father before he died. When our sister, Doreen, called to let me know he was sick and being treated at Straub in Honolulu, I quickly sorted my affairs and went. In the weeks leading up to his death, I sat by his bed, stroked his hair, talked to him. Mostly, just thanked him. For teaching me how to see and how to fight. For loving me fiercely and from the start. For calling me "son."

One of the greatest acts of my life was procuring the urn that would hold his ashes. When Doreen asked me to choose his urn, I knew it had to be lovely but simple. He would've wanted that. After an afternoon of avid searching, and with the help of a few good friends, I found it. A wooden

---

[36]The Paris Agreement enshrines the global goal to keep warming to "well below" 2 degrees Celsius above preindustrial levels. Many Pacific Islanders, convinced that target should be lower, started a campaign around the rallying cry, "1.5 to stay alive." To be sure, however, without rapid, far-reaching and unprecedented changes in all aspects of society, we're on course for a rise of 4-to-6 degrees, which, to be frank, would be cataclysmic. For further reading on this subject, I'd suggest Naomi Klein's incredible book, *This Changes Everything: Capitalism vs. The Climate*.

urn with a warm hue and a simple but stately inlay of mother-of-pearl. A fitting vessel for carrying the body of a beautiful soul to sea.

I'd like to end my remarks with a poem I wrote some time after that day at Tide Table. One of the things I loved most about our father was his ruthless insistence that young people (who take up the mantle of social justice work) realize that though we must respect those who came before us and cleared part of the path, we must also learn to trust ourselves to find our own way in the world.

That, and to remember that in the face of injustice, there is nothing more important than impatience.

Because the time for justice is always now.[37]

Because power concedes nothing without a demand.[38]

Frederick Douglass may have issued that reminder, but it is our father who never let us forget.

> Justice and
> Patience are
> not exactly
> friends
>
> but nobody knows this more
> than the Marshallese.

---

[37]From Dr. Martin Luther King, Jr.'s "Letter from Birmingham Jail."
[38]From Frederick Douglass's "West India Emancipation" speech.

They—

who watched the world turn red
and the rain turn into a terrorist

whose thyroids were taken as were their voices
but not the love of singing or the memory of song

who buried too many beautiful babies to count

who've been denied not only big things like
reparations, remediation and a promise of return
but little things too like arrowroot
flour and the flesh of coconut crabs

who waited for years by the seashore for
some small boat of deliverance to dock

—know the bitter truth.

Waiting is
Empire's
favorite
game
of
all

and
Patience

a parka
of loneliness

to wear on
an island with
no chance of
snow.

Gaosåli[39]

so much hope
for the future

rests in a
return to

the right
flower

to gaosåli

torchwood
of the sea

whose square
white flowers

cling to no one
but the rugged

---

[39]"Gaosåli" is dedicated to Judi Won Pat, who tried to change the official flower of Guam from the invasive bougainvillea to the native gaosåli and was mocked for it.

limestone
cliffs

at the
island's
edge

whose wood
warms us

whose wood
will light

our way
again.

Curved Sticks and Cowrie Shells: A Conversation between Julian Aguon & Desiree Taimanglo-Ventura

Desiree Taimanglo-Ventura is a former professor at Guam Community College, where she taught composition and communications. She is also a longtime friend of the author. The two met more than twenty years ago in the hallways of Simon Sanchez High School. The story goes, they hugged and never let go. Below is a lightly edited version of a conversation between Taimanglo-Ventura and Aguon in advance of the publication of the Guam edition.

DESIREE TAIMANGLO-VENTURA: I have a confession. The whole time I was reading your book I was thinking about that backpack you used to carry around in high school. The big-ass blue one. Then it shows up in *Nikki and Me*. Seeing it made me nostalgic with thoughts of young Julian, but then the image of it started to take on new meaning. As I was working my way through the book, I began to see the heaviness of it as more than literal. So, my first question, which I guess you could say is only about twenty years late, is what was even in there?

JULIAN AGUON: God knows! But that backpack was a safety blanket for sure. You know I never let it out of my sight, which is pretty hilarious now that I think of it because it's not like I had anything of any real value in there.

DESIREE: You never put it down! I could never figure it out because we barely had supplies or even textbooks we could take home. But yet, you always had so much to carry.

JULIAN: It was mostly just whatever I could get my hands on from the school library which, as you know, wasn't much. But I filled that sucker up anyway. Reading was an escape and an escape was something I needed. But wait. Did I ever tell you I fell down the stairs at school? I guess lugging that thing around every day was bound to catch up to me because one day, out of nowhere, I had a serious back spasm and fell backward down a whole flight of stairs. You know the staircase right after Mrs. Ruiz's office—the school nurse? That one. I die just thinking about it. It was so bad I had to get a shot of steroids in the butt. The whole scene was so extra.

DESIREE: I'm not at all surprised that you fell under the weight of that thing. But this is a side of you I think your readers don't really get to see in the book. I don't mean about you falling or getting an ass full of steroids, but this ability to laugh, at the world and at yourself, and to be joyful. Through all the grief and loss, you still laugh.

JULIAN: Oh, for sure. If you can't laugh, you're missing out on a hell of a lot. A human being is here to be enjoyed. Like a sunset or a tangerine. We're not oxen. We're not here to endlessly plow the earth. So yeah, we suffer, but we do so much more than that. You know what I keep thinking about? I keep thinking about what Toni Morrison said about racism. That the function of racism is distraction. That it keeps us from doing our work.

DESIREE: What work is that?

JULIAN: The work of turning our lives into art. She said that our lives are already artful, they're just waiting for us to make them art. So, the book in a way was an attempt to answer that call.

DESIREE: On that note, let's get into it. Because Julian, the book is really something. I think one of the best things about it is it does something that many people in our community don't do, or aren't comfortable doing, which is talk about our grief. But your book blows that wide open. It's like you're forcing us to the table to talk about things we don't want to talk about. Our individual and collective sense of loss. It really does seem like grief is the connective tissue that binds the book together. What was it like creating a space like that, to deal so directly with trauma?

JULIAN: You hit it on the head. The book's got grief in spades. In some of the pieces, like "Mugo," you get it all up front. You get it hard and fast. Then in others, like "No Country for Eight-Spot Butterflies," it creeps up all quiet like a house cat. But the grief is always there, lurking, roaming from room to room. But that's part of the point I'm making in the book. So much of our story as Indigenous peoples has been about shouldering enormous loss and pressing on anyhow, with our hearts broken and our eyes peeled for beauty. I think that's part of what the young Cree poet Billy-Ray Belcourt was saying with his collection, *This Wound is a World*, that Indigenous peoples have gone through some shit, but we're also able to engage the problems of the world without losing clarity about the futures we need to build.

DESIREE: Speaking of that, a lot of your pieces draw the reader's gaze toward those different ways of seeing and engaging. Sometimes you draw us close to show us something small like a grasshopper's legs. Then you'll do this thing where you'll use something else that is small or simple or mundane, like a cake, in order to make a point about something big. I'm thinking specifically of "Birthday Cakes Mean Birthdays," which I've used in my classroom and which always evokes strong reactions from the students. When you're writing, how much thought goes into making these kinds of connections between very small things and very big ones?

JULIAN: A lot actually. There's a paragraph in "Yugu Means Yoke" where I talk about finding "a whole wide world" on Mount Santa Rosa. I didn't even realize I had something here until I wrote that paragraph. To me, that paragraph is the whole beating heart of the book. A boy rolling around in red dirt and running through sword grass and getting cut up. And finding a family of slow-moving tree snails and wondering if they could ever move swiftly enough to save their own lives. It was such a vulnerable time in my life. But that's also the moment a writer is born.

DESIREE: That paragraph is really powerful. Actually, it was my favorite part of the book.

JULIAN: I like it also because it gets at something else Indigenous peoples understand—that land is life, and that we can't keep trampling over it because it contains the medicine we need to heal ourselves.

DESIREE: Your introduction says the book is a love letter to young people. But if you read it carefully, it's pretty obvious it's also a love letter to your favorite writers—writers many of our students may not know. So, was that part of your goal—to introduce them to these writers, to reference them like points of light?

JULIAN: Most definitely. In a way, I think I was just writing the book I wish I'd read. Being a womanist, or feminist of color, I had to give them at least a few of the amazing black women whose work is so foundational—Audre, Alice, Toni. And, of course, there are so many more who never made their way into the footnotes. Angela Davis, for example, is a force of nature. Even the title of "Fighting Words" was inspired by a black woman, Patricia Hill Collins. I first read her in undergrad when I was studying sociology at Gonzaga University. Speaking of points of light, to this day I still count my lucky stars I had a teacher as remarkable as Jane Rinehart. That woman was a gift. And the list just goes on. I also gave them some native writers I grew up reading. And you know there's this whole new wave of native writers that I wasn't able to include, but our kids should know about. Tommy Orange and Terese Mailhot are two that come to mind. So yes, you could say I felt an urgent need to offer these writers up.

DESIREE: Is there any writer from our region whom you especially love—or whose work you would want to direct our students to?

JULIAN: The Marshallese poet Kathy Jetñil-Kijiner. The first time I heard her, I was reminded of that South African proverb that goes, until lions write books, history will always glorify the hunter. I remember thinking, here's a lion with a pen.

DESIREE: Is there any piece in particular that really had an impact on you?

JULIAN: Kathy's probably at her best in these video poems, where you actually see and hear her delivering the lines. In "Tell Them," she's working with these impossibly gentle images, like shell earrings and woven baskets and braided girls cartwheeling in the rain. Then in "Anointed," she's walking on top of Runit Dome—a nuclear waste facility. A *leaking* nuclear waste facility. And she's doing the damn thing. Summoning language from the depth of her people's pain. And yeah, it's a poem, but it's also this whole historical indictment. And like a boss, she's reading every charge out loud. I don't know but, to me, it doesn't get any better than that.

DESIREE: The epigraph. Can we talk about that? It was so simple but also so subversive.

JULIAN: Look, there's nothing lovelier, there's nothing easier, than birdsong. But here's the catch: the brown tree snake has all but snuffed out that heavenly sound from our island. I mean, a whole generation has come up after us with no real memory of birdsong. That's sad. And, as with so many other invasive species, the snake was brought here by the United States and is one of those gifts from the colonizer that keeps on giving. And, of course, the whole sordid mess marches on, with the US military ripping still more limestone from the forest floor. It's not only the birds' habitat they're destroying, but also the hope we harbor for their homecoming.

DESIREE: You used footnotes as a way to sneak in all kinds of side conversations with the reader. Were there any other conversations you felt were important but ultimately abandoned for one reason or another?

JULIAN: In "Nikki and Me," I had a ridiculously long footnote that I worked on forever but ended up chucking in the eleventh hour. Anyway, it was this really heavy conversation about the many layers of Micronesian identity, which are exceedingly complex. So, I found myself explaining way too many things: Micronesia as one of the three subregions of Oceania, the delicate state of race relations between Chamorros and Chuukese in Guam, even the evolution of the entities we now know as Palau, the Marshall Islands, and the Federated States of Micronesia. All of it felt important, you know? First, because too many of our fellow Chamorros tend to forget that we too are Micronesians. Second, because we also tend to place a disproportionate amount of the blame on each other when, in reality, many of our grievances lie primarily with the United States. To be clear, some of our region's most intractable problems are irrefutably American in origin. Anyway, it became obvious that the whole thing had to go, as it would've bogged down the piece. And with that piece in particular, the point that mattered most was the simpler one: that there are times, especially in the presence of injustice, when we just have to act. Get up. Charge the bus. Even if we don't exactly know what we're doing.

DESIREE: One of my favorite passages in the book is from "Fighting Words." In it, you talk about music, about your grandmother's love of Aretha Franklin, about how you used to sing to her—your grandmother, that is, not Aretha. I was wondering. Did she ever sing to you, too? If so, what did she sing?

JULIAN: "You Are My Sunshine" was her go-to. But she also loved this simple number called "Pearly Shells," which she picked up from her time living in Hawai'i. She'd sing it whenever we'd go to the beach to swim or go hunting for seashells.

DESIREE: On another note, why don't you sing anymore? Seriously, singing was like your whole life growing up. I should threaten you with footage from back in the day. All the high school pep rallies. All the karaoke contests. Most of which you won by the way. But as an adult, you hardly ever sing, except maybe when someone close to you dies. What is up with that?

AGUON: I think I was just way better back then. I think *Sister Act 2* had just come out. And God knows that was reason enough. I loved that movie. "Joyful, Joyful" was my jam. In fact, it was my first solo in Mrs. Cabral's choir class. And it was the beginning of what would become one of my life's greatest love affairs. I'm speaking of course of my undying love for Ms. Lauryn Hill. *The Miseducation of Lauryn Hill* is one of the best albums of all time.

DESIREE: I have so many students who want to write but don't believe they can ever produce something for publication. This requires a lot of unpacking, as you can imagine. But it makes me think of your message in "The Ocean Within." I don't know if you realize this, but many of my students also went to our high school. The discussion that comes up after we read it as a group often ends up sounding like a kind of group therapy session. The students genuinely see themselves and their community in it. What would you say to the young writer who, like you, comes from our public school system and who, like you, came of age by way of struggle, by way of the village, by way of a red-dirt road? What would you say to her as she reads your book and dreams of one day writing her own?

AGUON: I would say I can't wait to read it. I would also encourage her to take to heart what the great Epeli Hau'ofa said about smallness. That smallness is a state of mind. For far too long, we in Micronesia, which literally means "small islands," have let outsiders do all kinds of framing for us—spatial, cultural, political. That's a death trap. The truth is there's nothing small about the greatness from which we come. We come from wayfinders. Seafarers who sliced through millions of miles of open ocean with little more than curved sticks and cowrie shells. An enormous map in their minds. One that accounted for every island and every swell of sea. Every bird and every star that shivers in the distance. If that's not magic, I don't know what is. So,

I'd tell her to draw close to that well, drink that water, then kindly bring someone else something to drink.

DESIREE: That's beautiful.

JULIAN: Lucky for us, beauty is something else we've got in spades.

I could not have anticipated how warmly this little book would be welcomed into the world. Written at the height of the pandemic, and primarily as a way to process my grief, it was released in the spring of 2021 under the title, *The Properties of Perpetual Light*. Unthinkably good things have happened since. Apart from selling thousands of copies (and launching tiny book clubs around the world in the process), the book did something more special: it turned grief, which is usually a wall, into a bridge—a bridge that brought me closer to other people, and other people closer to each other.

If it is true that a dam exists in every colonized people's heart, the book broke a part of it down. I know this because stories rushed out of my own people like a river. Friends and family called and wrote in droves. Strangers sent clandestine messages about their struggles—young people considering suicide, activists ground down by bitter defeats, medicine women, mental health counselors, mothers of gay sons. Folks showed up at my home bearing all manner of small gifts. A young weaver brought a handful of woven grasshoppers. A woman who knew my grandma brought bananas. A fisherman brought a cooler full of fish. Each of them brought stories of their own—stories of love and loss, of dreams and disappointment, of varying degrees of brokenheartedness. The stories that unspooled around me confirmed that Alice Walker was right when she said that the way forward is with a broken heart.

The book also fortified a friendship more than twenty years in the making. I have known Victoria-Lola Leon Guerrero, managing editor of the University of Guam Press, since high school, when we were both youth reporters for the local paper, but I had never worked closely with her.

Not close-close. The book changed that. I watched in awe as she carried it tenderly through every stage of the publishing process, from the first round of line edits to choosing the cloth for the inside cover. The only way to describe the devotion with which she does her work is love, which makes sense, as she single-handedly revived the island's only press after a 30-year dormancy. Without her, the book would not have been born.

I have been asked more than a few times (mostly by other writers) what one word I'd use to describe this book. If I had to choose, that word would be quiet. Because the work of confronting empire is almost always loud, part of me wanted to force the reader to have to lean in and listen. I am convinced that matters because, now more than ever, we need radical listening, which is to say listening to the voices of those more vulnerable than us, whose lives are more precarious than our own.

My people are doing that now.

We have our ears to the ground and we are listening to our eight-spot butterfly, whose forest home is being razed for a machine-gun range. We are doing what we can to save her. We are protesting. We are working to save the two rare plants whose leaves she lays her eggs on. We are suing US Fish and Wildlife Service on her behalf.

We are not naive. We know we might not win. But we also know we owe it to her to fight at least as hard as she does. Though far less famous than her sister, the monarch butterfly, she is just as strong, if not stronger. Whereas her sister goes through five larval instars, she goes through six. It stops my blood to think about that. She has to die six times in order to live.

So, when my new editor Danny Vazquez suggested we title this edition of the book *No Country for Eight-Spot Butterflies*, I dropped my shoulders because I knew he got it. I knew he understood the centrality of beauty in the struggle for collective liberation. I knew he knew the difference between strength and power. And that is the difference that will make a difference.

Looking ahead, I am filled with hope—and not the bullshit kind—but the kind that is earned, from struggle, in community. I will be writing about that earned hope in my next book, which sprung from an essay of mine that *The Atlantic* published on the opening day of COP26, entitled, *To Hell with Drowning*.

In the essay, I wove together stories from across Oceania about how climate change is impacting our peoples and how we are fighting back. I argued that in the fight against climate change—the fight of our lives—we will not win by way of facts. But we might by way of stories.

I may have started that argument in the essay, but I plan to finish it in the book.

—Julian Aguon
November 2021

REFERENCES

Aguon, J. (2008). *What We Bury at Night*. Tokyo: Blue Ocean Press.

Alexie, S. (1996). *Reservation Blues*. New York: Warner Books.

Ball, M. (1987). "Constitution, Court, Indian Tribes." *American Bar Foundation Research Journal*, 12(1), 1–140.

Burnett, C. D., & Marshall, B. (2001). *Foreign in a Domestic Sense: Puerto Rico, American Expansion, and the Constitution*. Durham, NC: Duke University Press.

Coelho, Paulo. (1993). *The Alchemist*. San Francisco: HarperOne.

Douglass, F. (1950). *West India Emancipation*, in P.S. Foner (Ed.), *The Life and Writings of Frederick Douglass, Vol. 2: Pre-Civil War Decade 1850–1860*. New York: International Publishers.

Erdrich, L. (1993). *Love Medicine*. New York: Harper Perennial.

García Márquez, G. (1978). *One Hundred Years of Solitude*. New York: Pan Books.

Harjo, J. (1996). *The Woman Who Fell From the Sky: Poems* (revised ed.). New York: W. W. Norton & Company.

Hau'ofa, E. (2008). 'Our Sea of Islands.' *We Are the Ocean: Selected Works*. Honolulu, HI: University of Hawai'i Press.

Hau'ofa, E. (1994). *Tales of the Tikongs*. Honolulu, HI: University of Hawai'i Press.

Jetñil-Kijiner, K. (2017). *Iep Jaltok: Poems from a Marshallese Daughter*. Tucson, AZ: University of Arizona Press.

Kesey, K. (1992). *One Flew over the Cuckoo's Nest*. New York: Penguin Putnam.

King, M. L. (1968). "Letter from Birmingham Jail." Atlanta, GA: Martin Luther King Jr. Center for Nonviolent Social Change.

Klein, N. (2014). *This Changes Everything: Capitalism vs. the Climate*. New York: Simon & Schuster.

Lorde, A. (1995). *The Black Unicorn: Poems* (reissue ed.). New York: W. W. Norton & Company.

Lorde, A. (2013). *Sister Outsider: Essays and Speeches* (Crossing Press Feminist Series ed.). Berkeley, CA: Ten Speed Press.

Morrison, T. (1979). Barnard College commencement speech.

Morrison, T. (2004). *Beloved* (reprint ed.). New York: Vintage International.

Morrison, T. (1970). *The Bluest Eye*. New York: Holt, Rinehart, & Winston.

Najafi, S., & Burnett, C. D. (2010). "Islands and the Law: An Interview with Christina Duffy Burnett." *Cabin Magazine*.

Neruda, P. (1993). *Twenty Love Poems and a Song of Despair*. San Francisco, CA: Chronicle Books.

Roy, A. (1997). *The God of Small Things*. New York: Random House.

Roy, A. (2019). *My Seditious Heart*. Chicago, IL: Haymarket Books.

Rumi, J. Barks, C. (1995). *The Essential Rumi* (C. Barks, trans.). New York: HarperOne.

Walker, A. (2003). *The Color Purple*. New York: Harvest/Harcourt, Inc.

Walker, A. (1984). *In Search of Our Mothers' Gardens: Womanist Prose*. New York: Harcourt Brace Jovanovich.

Walker, A. (2010). *Overcoming Speechlessness: A Poet Encounters the Horror in Rwanda, Eastern Congo and Palestine/Israel*. New York: Seven Stories Press.

ACKNOWLEDGMENTS

I'd like to give thanks to the following people, whose kindness and support have meant so much to me in the lead-up to this new edition:

Brooke Lehman, Lenika Cruz, Sarah Souli, Maya Soetoro, Khury Petersen-Smith, Jason Wu, Bing Liu, Jen Robinson, Tom Kruse, Christine Ahn, E. Tammy Kim, Jay Caspian Kang, Andy Liu, Rebecca McInroy, Tom Philpott, Raj Patel, Jamie McDonald Knapp, Jeremy Wang-Iverson, Wendy Miles, Maureen Penjueli, Katie Steinhaus, Sarah Sevedge, Sarah Flett Prior, Brendan Basham, Varsha Gandikota-Nellutla, Nikhil Dey, Aruna Roy, Nick Estes, Avi Lewis, Naomi Klein, Alice Walker, Kristin Casper, Annie Leonard, Derrick Muña Quinata, Rodney Jacob, Leevin Camacho, Sharleen Santos-Bamba, Katie Mafnas, Lisa Natividad, Autumn Bordner, Margaretha Wewerinke-Singh, Julie Hunter, Victoria-Lola Leon Guerrero and Desiree Taimanglo-Ventura.

I'd also like to thank:

Tommy Orange, for believing in me

Duvall Osteen, for having my back

Danny Vazquez, for making Astra House a home

Arundhati Roy, for honoring me with her incredibly beautiful introduction

And finally:

Ronald Reyes Gogo—for teaching me what his mother Josefa taught him—that to be Chamorro is to have blood in your eyes, which means to have compassion for kith and kin, and to never forget that the way of love is the way of reciprocity.

ABOUT THE AUTHOR

Julian Aguon is a Chamorro human rights lawyer and defender from Guam. He is the founder of Blue Ocean Law, a progressive firm that works at the intersection of Indigenous rights and environmental justice; and serves on the council of Progressive International—a global collective with the mission of mobilizing progressive forces around the world behind a shared vision of social justice. He lives in the village of Yona. Visit julianaguon.com.